GOD'S POWER WITHIN YOU

Attitudes for Living

PETER M. KALELLIS

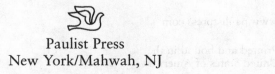

Paulist Press
New York/Mahwah, NJ

Cover Art: Sermon on the Mount, original icon designed in 2009 by George Filipakis. Used with permission.

Cover and book design by Lynn Else

Library of Congress Cataloging-in-Publication Data

Kalellis, Peter M.
    God's power within you : attitudes for living / Peter M. Kalellis.
        p. cm.
    Includes bibliographical references (p.   ).
    ISBN 978-0-8091-4655-0 (alk. paper)
    1. Beatitudes—Criticism, interpretation, etc. 2. Bible. N.T. Matthew V, 3–12—Criticism, interpretation, etc. I. Title.
    BT382.K36 2010
    226.9'306—dc22

                                                                    2010000237

Published by Paulist Press
997 Macarthur Boulevard
Mahwah, New Jersey 07430

www.paulistpress.com

Printed and bound in the
United States of America

CONTENTS

In loving memory of
Anna K. Bouras,
whose life reflected
the teachings of Christ
and whose presence touched many people
with genuine kindness and inspiration.
In her own gentle way, she encouraged me
to pursue my deep desire to write.
As Anna continues in God's grace,
we will remember her fondly and
thank God for her time among us.

ACKNOWLEDGMENTS

God's Power Within You: Attitudes for Living owes its life, form, and shape to Paul McMahon, the managing editor of Paulist Press. He gave this project at least twice as much time as anyone could have expected and made certain valuable suggestions that made the book a most inspirational reading.

I am grateful to—

- the editorial department of Paulist Press for comments and text improvements that made this effort worthwhile.

- Pat, my loving and patient wife of thirty-two years; she stands by me supportively as I obsess over writing another book. I am a lucky man, and I love her dearly.

- my four loving children—Katina, Mercene, Michael, and Basil—and my three grandchildren—Nikki, Andrew, and Stacey-Mercene—whose presence in my life has been the fountainhead of inspiration.

- my colleagues and coworkers, especially Margery Hueston and Pattie Manzi, who diligently edited the last draft.

God's Power Within You

- and the Reverend Fathers Paul C. Costopoulos,
  Stephen J. Callos, George A. Alexon, James
  Dokos, Stephen Kyriakou, Paul Kucynda,
  James Rousakis, and Joseph Samaan who
  appreciate my work and periodically invite me
  to their parishes to conduct weekend retreats.

PROLOGUE

It is not an exaggeration to say that we live in troubled times. Freedom-loving people are currently breathing the polluted air of anxiety. Evil has seeped into our world, and constant threats of terrorist activities disturb our peace. Why? Where did we go wrong?

Huge forces are fighting each other—good against evil, freedom against tyranny, believers against infidels—making life an emotional struggle. During this critical period, many people in the armed forces are in foreign lands fighting for democracy, freedom, and human rights.

I fail to understand this part of the human condition. Why must we have war to defend our freedom or to establish peace?

Whether we like it or not, we are all involved in the ongoing struggle for peace, and we fear annihilation. When our mind functions rationally, we seek acceptance, love, and freedom: gifts that a loving God wants for us. As I think of a loving God, my memory takes me to a little town on a Greek island where I lived for the first twenty years of my life. Instantly, I see myself in a class of forty students listening to our teacher Theodora, which in Greek means "God's gift." She taught all subjects, but she excelled in teaching music and songs, which always carried a moral or a spiritual message.

As she spoke, our young minds identified with Greek heroes and their marvelous feats. Theodora instilled in us a belief in a loving God—a God who makes our life possible, who takes a glance around the earth and sees us all. God cares for the harmony in the world and for our happiness. Initially, he sent prophets to teach us how to live a life of peace and prosperity. Eventually, God sent Christ, his only Son, to give us direction and to teach us how to *be* among his people.

Theodora managed to kindle our faith and inspire us, especially during Holy Week when our little Greek town became the city of Jerusalem. Our priest, Papavasile, reenacted the drama of the passion of Christ and everyone participated. As the priest chanted the gospel, our hearts palpitated as our minds visualized the actual crucifixion that took place on Good Friday.

The everlasting drama of Christ is a metaphor: In Christ, the presence of God in human form, we cherish abundant blessings and unconditional love. Yet among us there is always a Judas, the presence of evil, whose destiny is to destroy. As a result, we have agony, a torturous death, crucifixion. But after Good Friday comes Resurrection, joy. Evil may triumph for a while, but eventually it is defeated, and salvation is at hand.

In the search for what they believe is "salvation," many people pursue physical pleasures or various forms of self-gratification: *When I obtain this or when I'm free of that, then I will be okay.* Invariably, any earthly satisfaction that we seek—the accumulation of material wealth or physical pleasure—is short-lived. This mind-set creates the illusion of salvation. True salvation happens today—at this moment—and after life, it will continue to become complete in the presence of God.

True salvation is inner peace, love, and life in all its fullness. It is a state of freedom from fear, from suffering, from a

perceived insufficiency, and from all wanting, needing, grasp-
ing, and clinging. It is freedom from anxiety and compulsive
thinking, from negativity, and, above all, from past and future
concerns. True salvation is to feel within you the good that has
no opposite; the joy of being that depends on nothing apart
from God. It is to "know God," not as some superpower in
outer space, but as the ever-present life-giving Spirit.

If any changes are to occur in our afflicted world, each
one of us will have to respond to life with a spirit of humility and goodness. The "me, myself, and I" perception will
have to be modified to include other people who suffer in
this world, those who have needs and deserve a decent life.
We need an *"other-centered"* attitude that promotes caring
for others as we care for ourselves.

This book explores our potential offered by Christ in
his Sermon on the Mount—commonly known as the
Beatitudes. Each of the Beatitudes (Be–attitudes) begins with
the word *blessed*. In Greek, the word *blessed* is *makarios*,
which means *a person who has found absolute happiness
and serenity within*. Our use of *makarios* (blessed) here
denotes a state of contentment, inner joy, exuberance, which
a person experiences in living a godly life.

Throughout the nine Beatitudes, Christ summarizes his
teachings about life and explains how we should *be* as children of God. Each brief statement suggests qualities that
help us become members of the kingdom of heaven. This
desired state of happiness in the kingdom of heaven is not an
abstract or indefinite promise. It is a reality that starts in our
present life and provides inner joy and peace while we are
still in this world. Ultimate happiness, which will be our
reward in heaven, may be best described by St. Paul:

What no eye has seen, nor ear heard, nor the human heart conceived, what God has prepared for those who love him. (1 Cor 2:9)

Introduction
AN INVITATION

The beginning of a happier, healthier, and more rewarding life can occur at any moment. In Joseph's case, this moment was brought on by an invitation. Joseph, a forty-seven-year-old businessman, had worked hard since the age of fourteen. He had previously been to seven other therapists before coming to seek my help.

"No one can help me," he said in a sad voice. "I'm a failure."

Joseph enumerated his problems, emphasizing painful details. His wife had decided to leave him, his two sons went with their mother and didn't want to see him, and his computer software business was failing.

"I have been unhappy all my life," he said. "I tried to convince myself that tomorrow things would get better, but that never happened. I keep on going in the hope of seeing a light at the end of the tunnel, but I haven't seen it yet."

"So, hope is what keeps you going?" I asked.

"Hope is what brought me to your office. Hope for a better tomorrow."

"What about today? Don't you want to feel better today?"

"Of course I do, but I feel stuck because of the bad choices I have made in my life."

1

"Suppose you put your bad choices aside for a while and focus on the hour that you are here with me."

"My past is always before me, haunting me. How can I forget it?"

"Joseph, I'm not asking you to forget it. There is not much that we can do about your past, but you can learn from the lessons it taught you."

Joseph, like most therapy seekers, was plagued with anger, guilt, regret, resentment, grievances, sadness, bitterness, and all forms of blame. As he identified with such negative thinking, he saw no way out.

I looked him straight in the eye, and said, "If you use the rest of this hour to tell me all your problems, you are leaving no room for anything new to enter, no room for a solution."

"Our priest told me that you are a Christian therapist, and you may be the one who can help me."

I saw hope in his eyes. I clarified my position as a therapist and explained that I did not operate a spa with his choice of amenities. What I did offer was an invitation to challenge his awareness of life. He could learn how to coordinate thoughts, feelings, and behaviors, how to leave the past behind, and how to make space to allow God to enter his life's situation.

This invitation involved his acceptance of God's gift of grace, as evident in the words of Saint Paul: "*For by grace you have been saved through faith, and this is not your own doing; it is the gift of God—not the result of works, so that no one may boast*" (Eph 2:8–9).

Furthermore, the invitation involved having his faith in Jesus Christ—in Jesus' miraculous birth, exemplary life, painful death, and glorious resurrection. Jesus is God's way of bringing joy and salvation to the world. We have faith that Jesus is ever-present in our lives as Lord and Savior, as Teacher and Friend, to guide our earthly life—and as a Companion and Helper to protect us from going astray. We have faith that our lives have meaning and purpose and that we are not alone in the struggle for survival. God is the powerful, benevolent force at work in the world, and despite the fears, obstacles, and uncertainties of the present life, we should not be afraid, for God is in charge.

The invitation also implies entering into an intimate, living, loving, and eternal relationship with God the Father, through Jesus Christ the Son, by the power of the Holy Spirit. Christ is life, the source of life, the source of joy, the source of the true light, nurturing us with his teachings. He offers true love that transforms us into different and happier people. With Christ in our hearts, our thoughts and actions change. Our passions subside. We are no longer able to do evil or to hate or to seek revenge. It is through his grace that we can endure adversities. Sadness, illness, pressure, anxiety, or even depression cannot defeat us.

As we are instructed in the Gospel of Matthew: "*Obey everything that I have commanded you. And remember, I am with you always, to the end of the age*" (Matt 28:20). While obeying everything may appear to be an impossible goal, Christ made it attainable for us. At the very beginning of his ministry, Jesus delivered the Sermon on the Mount, which contains the Beatitudes (Matt 5:3–11), the most concise and practical outline of spiritual truth known to humanity. The Beatitudes summarize a major part of the Christian faith.

Notice that Jesus does not commence by saying, "You shall not do this," or, "You shall not do that," which are restrictive statements. That was the style of the Law and the prophets, which underlined conformity to external practices, such as keeping the Sabbath, fasting, or observing Passover.

Rather, Jesus enters the inner essence of the human soul. He does not speak of conforming but of transforming.

Saint Paul reflects this ideal when he says, *"Do not be conformed to this world, but be transformed by the renewing of your minds"* (Rom 12:2). This invitation to change our way of thinking is reflected in Psalm 51:10: *"Create in me a clean heart, O God, and put a new and right spirit within me."* These verses present a good attitude for living. But what is attitude? It is a manner of thinking, feeling, and acting. It is an inner response that reveals our disposition or explains our behavior. Our attitude can be our best friend or our worst enemy. With a clean heart, let's apply the attitude offered by our Lord. We can be in this world, but we don't have to comply with all that contemporary society seems to demand of us. The fish that lives in the ocean all its life never gets salty.

The old Law taught people what to do, but Jesus showed them how to *be*, how to think, and how to interact with the world around them. His teaching is simple, direct, and practical. It requires awareness of who we truly are; it requires faith in God, the Giver of Life; it requires discipline.

As we let go of the attachments and aversions that we bring with us from early childhood but are impractical in adulthood, we begin to sense the presence of God in our daily life and feel unconditionally accepted, forgiven, loved, happy, and secure. It is his love and grace that makes all this possible.

Christ offers a pure "blessedness," a state of happiness beyond fame, fortune, and possessions. However, we cannot simply be passive receivers. We have to be active participants in his plan. This effort is a key with which to open the door to a healthier "attitude" and to redirect our attention to a happiness that is infinitely more profound and satisfying than any fleeting pleasures. It is our choice.

4

Happiness does not necessarily mean "good fortune." Rather, it is a state of being blessed; being on the path the Creator intends for us (keeping in mind that a blessing for one who believes may appear to be an affliction to a nonbeliever).

Blessed means something consecrated or belonging to God. The passages in Matthew where the word *blessed* appears is a translation from the Greek verb *makarios*. The plural form, *makarioi*, is used throughout the Beatitudes. The state of being blessed is the most awesome and sacred gift that God offers us, as we become aware of the redeeming activity of Christ's presence in our life. This blessing is our invitation to intimacy with Christ, the ultimate joy.

MEDITATION

Lord Jesus, show me the way!

In order to appreciate God's invitation, we must possess the right attitude. To have a good relationship with God, we must be receptive, appreciative, and humble.

"Let us come before his presence with thanksgiving" (Ps 95:2).

Being caught up in the currents of today's culture makes living in this relationship difficult. Let us be attentive to our Lord's ways, follow in his footsteps, and benefit from his divine wisdom.

1

THE POOR IN SPIRIT

With power and simplicity, Jesus sets forth spiritual principles that have echoed undiminished through the ages, tenets by which humans become blessed and filled with lasting joy.

When Jesus saw the crowds, he went up the mountain, and after he sat down, his disciples came to him. *He sat down*—this is significant. Sitting down was the normal posture of a teacher in the classical world. This detail indicates that the teaching was formal, not casual. Jesus was about to explain the principles of living in the kingdom of God—a state of blessedness in the presence of God.

Blessed are the poor in spirit, for theirs is the kingdom of heaven.

What is poverty of spirit? The Apostle Paul says *"not to think of yourself more highly than you ought to think, but to think with sober judgment"* (Rom 12:3). We gain a better understanding of poverty when we think of the poverty of Christ. Although he is God, he took on human form, associated with the poor, and connected with sinners; he chose poverty and endured dishonor; he brought freedom, accepted the plight of a prisoner, and was led in chains to be judged by the lawless, a maddened and murderous mob whose aim was to please the authorities.

The root word that is translated as *spirit* is more accurately translated as *pride*—poor in pride. It does not mean material poverty. It does not mean lack of brains. Rather, it suggests humility. Jesus says, *"Theirs is the kingdom of heaven,"* implying that heaven consists of humble people.

Humble people are those who acknowledge God as the Giver of All Blessings, and who are not impressed with material possessions. Their joy is a result of self-knowledge. They are aware of their situation, they know they are not perfect, and they accept their vulnerability.

Humble people know to follow the right path and seek God's help when they fail. Jesus humbled himself, therefore, humility implies obedience to God. It is humility that will bring us to heaven where there is peace and joy in the presence of God.

Ouranos is the Greek word for "heaven." The plural form, *ouranoi*, means "many heavens," an "infinite expansion." Jesus refers to the expanding potential within each individual. If we turn to the gospels, we discover that Jesus came *"not to abolish but to fulfill"* (Matt 5:17). Heaven is not simply a particular place in the sky or a reward given in the afterlife. Heaven is the potential of the Spirit in each one of us. It is the inner feeling of joy that Jesus is present in our life. When Jesus says, *"The kingdom of heaven is within you,"* he implies that the kingdom which God has planned for us starts here and now and continues in the life after our physical death.

Intellectually, the concept may be difficult to conceive. Our human minds cannot define God. Theologians and great scholars have tried, but no one has ever succeeded in describing the reality of God and his wisdom. God is infinite, beyond all comprehension and description. It is for this reason—God becoming man and going through the stages of human development—that we humans can understand his love and his ultimate plan for us. In the context of humility, we come closer to God when we believe and understand the meaning of Jesus' words, *"Blessed are the poor in spirit."*

We are blessed when we let go of our attempts to intellectualize the Bible and God's presence in our life and creation. How significant is Jesus' statement, *"Let the little children come to me, and do not stop them; for it is to such as these that the kingdom of heaven belongs"* (Matt 19:14). Children are pure, innocent, teachable, open-minded, and receptive to the truth.

Learning is a lifetime process. As long as we are alive, we can continue to learn. As we learn new information, we can abandon preconceived opinions and notions. Advanced science and technology provide a wealth of information that computers bring into our homes. As our knowledge increases, our ego is often inflated, allowing pride to get in our way. We ignore the fact that our intellect is God's gift to us—the vehicle he has given us to be his co-creators in the world. Yet, this great gift of intelligence is often misused. Instead of creativity, it brings about corruption, distorted beliefs, and catastrophe.

For example, mass media inundates our life daily with graphic and realistic details about drugs, murders, and violence. Most people become stressed as they view today's news or as they become lured by the cleverly seductive advertisements that may result in unnecessary purchases and debt. Millions of dollars are invested annually to produce soft-core porn and other materials that victimize young vulnerable minds and destroy their potential for mature thinking and growth. Hollywood, the mecca of the movie industry, produces some violent and degrading movies under the guise of entertainment. Unthinkingly, we become victims of the

9

"Everybody has it" mentality, or we become apathetic and ask, "What can *I* do? This is the world we live in."

Most of our activities or busy schedules are a means to an end. Fulfillment is always just around the corner or confined to short-lived pleasures of food, drink, drugs, or sex. We become focused on becoming, achieving, and attaining, or, alternately, chasing a new thrill or pleasure. Our fantasy is that if we acquire more belongings, we will become more fulfilled and psychologically complete. Perhaps if we win the lottery and become millionaires, our life will be at its best ever. Under such an illusion, we ignore that all these things—fame, riches, and glory—are pure vanity and vanish after death.

An old-fashioned attitude to truth can be helpful. Truth is not an intellectual grasp of scientific or metaphysical principles. It is an inward revelation that requires faith and conviction that there is a God who cares for us. We are not accidents of fate or the result of evolution. We came from God, and some day we will return to God. With such a foundation, we appreciate and respect life and move on with a sense of joy and gratitude to the Giver of Life.

We live in God's world, and yet in recent years, arrogance, pride, and evil make concerted attempts to chase God away. Imagine that your father gives you a home to live in and enjoy; later, this becomes your property. You take good care of this home and proudly admit that this is your inheritance. Suddenly someone shows up and forcefully tries to evict you. He arrogantly commands, "You cannot live here anymore." He wants to take over your house and make it his own.

Isn't this similar to what is progressively happening in our times? The creator and owner of this world is pushed out of our life. How familiar we are with the current political correctness to please all minorities and variety of political, religious, or social groups. Years ago, the long tradition of offering a morning prayer in the classroom was totally eliminated. Gradually, God's name was removed from our schools. The nativity scene, which for decades created a joyful spirit during Christmas, can no longer appear in many public areas. Innocent greetings such as "Merry Christmas" and "Happy Easter" have been replaced by "Happy Holidays." What has happened to the freedom of expression that is God's gift? Why do we accept such blandness that ignores the divinity of Christ?

Is faith in God an obstacle or a tool of comfort, encouragement, and strength? Some people restrict God to church on Sundays. However, we do like God to be around in difficult times or during sickness. We question his presence at the time of serious illness or death of a loved one. But we don't have time or room for him during work or pleasant times. These are parts of our lives we think we can, and think we should, handle on our own.

A growing body of research is making it clear that religion can be linked to superior mental health. This idea may come as a surprise to many in the modern psychiatric community that, still following in the footsteps of Freud, has long regarded religious behavior as, at best, a dependent state and as, at worst, a pathological condition. For example, as late as 1994 the American Psychiatric Association officially classified *strong religious beliefs* as a mental disorder (DSM-IV, 1994).

New data, however, indicates that religious beliefs and practices can improve mental and emotional health in several significant ways. For example, research shows that rates of drug abuse, alcoholism, divorce, and suicide are much lower among religious individuals than among the population at large. It also seems clear that people who genuinely

11

practice their faith are much less likely to suffer from depression and anxiety than those who are lax in their faith. Furthermore, the religious group recovers more quickly when they do suffer from depression and anxiety.

In the year 1999, researcher Dr. Harold Koenig of Duke University Medical Center, in reviewing more than a thousand studies on the impact of religion upon health, arrived at an impressive conclusion: "Men and women who are committed to their faith have fewer strokes, less heart disease, better immune system function, and lower blood pressure than the population at large. Lack of religious involvement has an effect on mortality that is equivalent to forty years of smoking one pack of cigarettes per day."

It is evident that Dr. Koenig's conclusion refers to religious beliefs in general. As Christians, we believe that Jesus Christ is the physician of bodies and souls and the ultimate healer. Physically or mentally ill people find comfort in their faith in Christ. They experience *something* beyond human intervention taking place. Individuals and families undergoing critical times travel long distances to find help at Christian shrines, monasteries, and convents. Many return to their homes totally cured. Others find relief and gradual healing.

One of the major aspects of the Christian faith is its power to alleviate pain and existential stress by granting us a sense of empathy with and strength over an uncertain and terrifying world. We believe that relief and healing are made possible by the presence of God. The ever-present, yet invisible power of God is tapped through faith and prayer. It is faith that offers believers the assurance that their lives have meaning and purpose, that they are not alone in the struggle of survival.

In spite of our distorted and self-damaging attitudes, God does not go away. He continues to be present in our lives. Can we ignore the fact that this world is created by God? We are God's tenants. He is the source of our life. He gives us breath, makes our hearts beat, and keeps us functioning each day. Whatever we accomplish, whatever possessions or positions we attain in our life, they are made possible because our Lord has endowed us with the ability, energy, intellect, and strength to achieve them. In the words of Saint Paul, "*I can do all things through him who strengthens me*" (Phil 4:13).

If we accept this with gratitude, then, like the trapeze artist, we can abandon the familiarity and security of what holds us back, free ourselves from any other distraction and multiplicity, and reach out with faith and gratitude to the firm grasp of God.

How interesting is the story of the rich ruler who came to Jesus and said, "*Good Teacher, what must I do to inherit eternal life?*" Something was obviously missing in his busy life. He was interested in the teachings of Jesus and wanted to be one of his followers. In essence, Jesus told him to sell all his possessions, give the money to the poor, and then come back and join him. We are told that the young man "*became sad; for he was very rich*" (Luke 18:18–23).

The man missed the point. Jesus did not mean that one must give up all one's wealth and be poor to be his follower. He referred to the possessions of the mind, the mental baggage that the man carried. His problem was not his material possessions. Most likely he was loaded with distorted ideas, perceptions of life and living, false values, and pride in his achievements, including the notion that riches were the key to his security and happiness. In reality, he was not in charge of his possessions; his possessions controlled his life and he felt chained to them. Jesus simply tested him to see if he was ready to walk the path of discipline of mind and spirit. Had the man said, "Teacher, I'll do as you wish," Jesus might have told him to keep what he had and acknowledge God as the source of whatever he possessed.

"*Blessed are the poor in spirit for theirs is the kingdom of heaven*" has deep meaning. When we release the imprisoned splendor of the spirit within and let go of our mental baggage, we rediscover God's abundant love for us.

MEDITATION

Our First Be-attitude

Jesus enters our life today with a unique purpose: to redeem us from the adversities of this world, to forgive our sins, to heal our suffering, to comfort us, and to give us freedom, joy, and a new direction. He loves and accepts us unconditionally. He imparts to us, without any effort on our part, the spirit of kindness. How different our life becomes when we follow his path.

Lord Jesus, take away from us the spirit of pride.

Lord, it is with genuine gratitude for what I already have in my life, and with deep humility, that I ask for the outpouring grace of your daily blessings. Amen.

2

THE MOURNERS

The verb *mourn* in the New Testament is translated from the Greek word *penthountes*, meaning "heartbreaking sorrow." It is the feeling of anguish over the loss of someone loved and desperately missed. Physical pain, suffering, and death are inevitable parts of life, and the survivors go through a period of grief. Tears relieve those who grieve; crying pours out the poisons of pain. Relief comes to those who allow their hearts to connect with Christ and identify with the *wounded healer* who endured excruciating pain on the cross—the price that he paid for the sins of the world.

Blessed are those who mourn, for they will be comforted.

Our struggles and frustrations, defeats and disappointments, are part of humanity's perpetual quest for truth, for wisdom, for inner freedom, and for happiness.

Our conscience may bother us for the wrongs we have committed. As we mourn about unhappy events in our life that keep nagging our conscience, we have the opportunity to repent and ask God to forgive us. King David, regretting his past sins of adultery and murder, appealed to God for mercy: *"I know my transgressions, and my sin is ever before me....Create in me a clean heart, O God, and put a new and right spirit within me"* (Ps 51:3, 10).

As we regret our past failures and repent, God's love provides comfort, forgiveness, and peace of mind. His wisdom instills courage and confidence in our hearts:

> Turn back to the Lord and forsake your sins;
>   pray in his presence and lessen your offense....
> How great is the mercy of the Lord,
>   and his forgiveness for those who return to him!
> For not everything is within human capability.
>   (Sir 17:25, 29–30)

Regardless of our emotional or physical condition, we have the ability to turn to God, seek his mercy, dwell in the light, and enjoy life.

This is an invitation to an endless spiritual adventure. In brief, it is the transformation of our being into a refined person possessing faith and spiritual values, and exerting a persistent effort to apply them in everyday life. As a result, we will feel God's power within to help us withstand any adversities in life.

As we become aware of our errors, feel inner turmoil, and have sleepless nights and daily anguish, we go through a period of mourning. In such times, if we feel inner strength to endure our condition, we will feel comforted. Psalm 51 speaks eloquently of King David's remorseful heart. He had committed adultery and murder, and as he realized his grievous sins, he turned to God and cried:

> Have mercy on me, O God,
>   according to your steadfast love;
> according to your abundant mercy
>   blot out my transgressions.
> Wash me thoroughly from my iniquity,
>   and cleanse me from my sin.

> For I know my transgressions,
>   and my sin is before me always.
>   (Ps 51:1–3)

We often hear well-intentioned preachers telling their congregation that suffering paves the road to Heaven and that such a belief is part of the Christian faith. Did Jesus really say that it is necessary to experience sorrow and tragedy that we may be comforted? Could he mean that comfort comes as we become aware of the divine aspect of our physical self, the power within each person to endure pain? Could he mean that he will give us the needed strength during our time of trouble?

Granted, sorrow and troubles brought about by bad choices or wrong thinking can serve as useful lessons. At times, when we face a tragedy, when we lose a person we dearly love, when we suffer through accidents or natural catastrophes, or when we hear of terrorism and war, we become anxious. We regress, and like children, we complain. We cry. We need someone to rescue us. We get angry. We want answers. Why should a three-year-old child die? Why should parents lose their only son or daughter? Why does sudden death strike down a newly married woman, who leaves behind the man she married and a two-year-old child? Is it fair for this child to grow up without a mother? Why does God, who is supposed to love us, allow these terrible things to happen? These questions have no logical answer.

When America experienced the 9/11 tragedy, causing thousands of sudden deaths and leaving thousands of wounded hearts, Mercene, my oldest daughter, asked me that same question, "Dad, where was God? Why did he not stop those cruel people from causing so many deaths?" Similarly, can we blame God, the Giver of All Blessings, for

17

allowing the war in Iraq and Afghanistan to continue? Can we expect God to interfere with the choices we make?

God gave people free will; some people use it to do good, and others use it to do evil. My mind raises another question: *Why did God allow his only Son to suffer such a tragic death?* As I pondered my own question, my faith rescued me instantly from possible doubt about God's love. *"For God so loved the world that he gave his only begotten Son that those who believe in him should not perish but have everlasting life"* (John 3:16).

My faith reassures me that Christ is always present in our life. He was there at the Twin Towers catastrophe, once again crucified, co-suffering with the victims of human cruelty. He embraced and received the unfortunate ones as they passed through the valley of death, comforted their grieving relatives and strengthened those brave hearts, who at the risk of losing their own lives, made heroic efforts to help others to survive.

In front of the tomb of his friend Lazarus in Bethany, *"Jesus began to weep"* (John 11:35). He could have chastised Mary and Martha for their lack of faith. "Why are you so upset? Don't you know that I have power to raise the dead?" It was with compassion that he said, *"I am the resurrection and the life. Those who believe in me, even though they die, will live"* (John 11:25). Jesus' love is not detached nor dry-eyed nor oblivious to human mortality.

That Jesus wept is not simply a documented historical event that took place two thousand years ago. Jesus *weeps* for the condition of the world today. He is ever present in our lives. He shares our joys and wants us to be *blessed* and, therefore, happy. He shares our sorrows and provides comfort, direction, and healing.

Even as believing Christians, when our back is against the wall, we may begin to doubt God's love. Why? Because we

18

are ordinary people! There are moments of disbelief when we even question God's existence. Like little children whose parents have gone, we feel abandoned and scared. Christ felt the same way on the cross: *"My God, my God, why have you forsaken me?"* (Matt 27:46). In his human nature, he too felt abandoned and alone in his pain.

Jesus endured the most humiliating and painful death for a reason. It was his way of telling us that suffering is the reality of life. Personally, I wonder whether the death of Christ is of any comfort to people who suffer. Two of my lifetime friends experienced the ultimate pain; they witnessed the death of their children. Frank lost two sons; Athena lost her only son. When I spoke to Frank, the dialogue went like this:

"I lost my seventeen-year-old son in an accident. Why did my second son have to suffer a slow death by cancer at twenty-eight, leaving behind a pregnant wife? I'm angry at God. Why did he allow death to take both of my boys at such an early age?"

"Frank, honestly I don't know the answer."

"Is that how God shows his love?"

I had a hard time referring to the second beatitude, *"Blessed are those who mourn, for they will be comforted."* All I could do was pray for him and his wife.

The next time I visited Frank, he looked revitalized and in better spirits. He talked about visiting his sons at the cemetery; he talked to them and prayed that they were in a place free from pain or sorrow, a place of peace. When I asked him to tell me how he was feeling, he said, "I feel better. I have a busy schedule. I lecture in different parts of the country on suffering as being part of life. I explain that most of the time it cannot be avoided, and that it needs to be faced.

19

"During the week, I go to my church when nobody is there. In silence, I look at the cross and there I find the greatest comfort, meditating about the last days of Jesus. I visualize his crucifixion, how every part of his body endured pain: his head bleeding from the crown of thorns, his face dripping with spittle from the crowd, his cheeks bruised from the blows, his lips smarting from the bitter taste of vinegar mixed with gall, his ears listening to the blasphemers, his back striped with the scourging, his body stretched on the cross, his limbs nailed to the wood, and his side pierced with the lance. If Jesus, the Son of God, who brought into our corrupt world compassion, forgiveness, and unconditional love, suffered for our sake so he could free us from suffering, how long can I say, 'Why me, Lord?'"

"You are a man of faith," I said.

"Faith in Christ is my source of comfort."

My dialogue with Athena was different. She was a woman of great faith who invested a lifetime doing charity and educating people.

"My son was such a good boy; he was kindhearted and very talented. He was my joy and comfort. Why did God take him from me?" Painful tears escaped her eyes.

Empathetically I looked at the grieving mother. What comforting words could I offer? Silently, I listened. Between tears and smiles, she told me a number of stories about her son's growing years, his ambitions and dreams. Then her sad eyes turned to me. "When I look at the Mother of Jesus, I feel close to her. I can imagine how she must have felt, seeing her Son naked, a condemned man hanging on the cross."

Most families endure painful events. There is injustice, hypocrisy, selfishness, cruelty, greed, revenge, and lack of love and compassion in our imperfect world. These undesirable aspects are real and life is full of them. Yet we need to

20

know the meaning and the truth about life just as we need love. Both truth and love are attributes of God that can only be understood through faith, and faith is not an intellectual attribute. It is an activity of the soul. Sorrow and despair over a painful event disturb our peace. It is then that our soul seeks healing; faith paves the path to such healing. Faith in a God of love and compassion helps us to cope as we go through personal, physical, or emotional pain, or as we grieve a loved one's death. Faith and trust in God gives our thoughts a calm and healthy perspective in harmony with his will. "*Thy will be done*" is a daring and powerful reliance on God, yet this is what Jesus told us to do when we pray.

In moments of loneliness, we seek from relatives and strangers what we can no longer find in a personal faith. Psychotherapists cannot afford to say, "I cannot help you. This matter goes beyond my field of competence." What are our choices? When psychological or scientific knowledge fails, we turn our eyes toward God. In the depth of our inner self, among the crevices of desires and hopes, lingers a particle of God—*apospasma Theou*, the divine part of our human nature, our soul. When the existence of our soul is ignored, we hesitate to connect with God, and we hesitate to trust in his power that comforts, heals, and directs our life. Yet it is this hesitation, like the baby's hesitation taking its initial steps and learning to walk, that initiates our first steps toward God.

Understandably, in a materialistic environment we often ignore our divine potential. Our cluttered surroundings prevent us from seeing the words of Christ:

"Do not worry about your life,...or about your body....Look at the birds of the air; they neither sow nor reap nor gather into barns, and yet your heav-

21

enly Father feeds them. Are you not of more value than they? And can any of you by worrying add a single hour to your span of life?" (Matt 6:25–27)

If God has created a most beautiful world for our physical existence and wants us to be happy and makes possible every breath we take and every heartbeat we feel, would he not also be mindful of our pain during troubled times? Take a deep breath, exhale, empty your mind of negative thoughts, and pause for a moment. Visualize Christ standing before you with open arms, ready to embrace you and to hold you. Rest in his loving arms and feel his protective presence.

It is God's presence and healing force that is ceaselessly working to establish wholeness. The real question is: Do we want to get well? This was the same question that Jesus asked a man who had been a paralytic for thirty-eight years and who waited for a miracle by the pool at Bethsaida: "*Do you want to be made well?*" (John 5:1–9). Why would the healer ask a suffering person such a question? Is it because, for some people, it is a pleasure to be ill? Some patients find security in their illness. They find it interesting and profitable to get attention and receive sympathy for their pain. Others subconsciously use illness to escape from life's responsibilities.

Visualize Jesus approaching the paralytic and asking, "Do you want to be healed badly enough to give up your feelings of self-pity, to reject the longstanding habit of dwelling in despair and despondency, to be satisfied living without the attention and assistance and sympathy of others? Are you willing to take charge of the power that is within you?"

The moment a person in pain is able to say with faith, "I will be well," the body, mind, and soul cooperate to pursue healing. What truly helps is quiet and persistent prayer to the One who heals our bodies and souls. God provides healing not because we are worthy or saintly. He heals because it is his nature to heal and restore health to the afflicted. In times of tears and grieving, despair and helplessness, we may come to experience Christ's presence in our life.

God does not send problems or want us to experience deep mourning so that we may find happiness in heaven. Our vulnerability is subject to our being conditioned by mass media's offer of "instant relief." We resist the potential of gradual growth and maturity that are God's endowment to every human being. It may well be that when a serious problem comes to us, it is a fortuitous blessing because it leads us to stir up the gift of the Holy Spirit within and make us aware of Christ's presence in our life.

This awareness aroused something in the thief's heart, as he was dying on the cross next to Christ and said: *"Jesus, remember me when you come into your kingdom."* Christ's reply made the difference. *"Today, you will be with me in Paradise"* (Luke 23:42–43). When anguish clouds our minds and we feel alone, Jesus Christ is present. Beyond medical, psychological, or scientific intervention, there is his promise of resurrection.

MEDITATION

Our Second Be-attitude

The pangs of sorrow suffered by the ordinary person arise from the loss of human love, material possessions, or the nonfulfillment of earthly aspirations. When we genuinely regret the wrongs we do in our life, we find comfort in God.

Lord Jesus, bring comfort to my soul.

Lord Jesus, healer of bodies and souls, I am grateful for my life in spite of the challenges and difficulties that lead me beyond my abilities to cope. Extend your hand and bring me closer to you. You are the God of comfort and hope, the God of my salvation. Amen.

3

THE MEEK

It seems ironic that we need to be meek and humble to obtain a major inheritance. A business owner or a Wall Street executive might ask, "Are you kidding me?" A university professor may smile and say, "I'm really proud of my position. I worked for it." Truly, there is nothing wrong with feeling proud of worthwhile accomplishments. Yet, frequently we hear that to get ahead in life you need to be aggressive. The average person has many discouraging moments; he or she experiences the injustices of life where the least deserving seem to get the breaks.

Blessed are the meek, for they will inherit the earth.

Meekness is not weakness. It is a humble attitude that expresses itself in patient endurance during difficult times or serious encounters. Meekness implies leniency and always uses its resources appropriately, unlike the out-of-control emotions that are so often destructive and have no place in our life as believers.

The concept of humility is presented convincingly in the gospel story about two men, a tax collector and a Pharisee, who went to the temple to pray. Jesus, in response to their different attitudes, made a statement about the quality and the effect of their prayer: *"I tell you, this man went down to his home justified rather than the other; for all who exalt themselves will be humbled, but all who humble themselves will be exalted"* (Luke 18:14). Jesus points out that the weak are strong and the lowly are exalted. His divine wisdom implies neither a worldly success nor an accumulation of material wealth. It promises a healthy state of mind, which God makes available to anyone who is humble and grateful.

In our moral and spiritual quest, the most dangerous place of all is the church. As we look across the aisle—seeking reassurance about ourselves, judging others—that aisle can become a fatal pitfall. The translation of the parable does a minor injustice to the tax collector. He does not call himself "a sinner" in the original Greek; he calls himself *ton amartolon—the* sinner. He has not merely done wrong. He *is* wrong. Here we see a desperate, helpless man, in his own mind beyond redemption, who throws himself in total trust into the hands of God.

After the social and political revolutions of the midsixties and the late seventies, self-deification, known as *hubris* to the ancients, came to a halt. The "me, myself, and I" mentality proved to be an empty and joyless attitude that resulted in disappointment. In the middle of this emotional turmoil, the dawn of a promising new era surfaced and with it came a search for spirituality. Desperate and restless minds with good intentions went in different directions, searching for peace and stability. Gurus, teachers, and sages offered relief through New Age ideas, including styles of meditation, weekend retreats, and spiritual reading materials. The pundits of a godless psychology influenced innocent and naive minds to pursue whatever means gave them pleasure. But the desperate search for happiness cannot be found outside oneself.

Pope Gregory the Great was a man of genuine humility, who was called *servus servorum Dei,* "the servant of the servants of God"—a title later used for all popes. Pope Gregory divided sins into seven categories. These seven categories have come to be known as the seven deadly sins or the seven cardinal sins. They are pride, covetousness, lust, envy, gluttony, anger, and sloth. It is natural to ask why Pope Gregory put pride at the top of the list. Why not anger or lust? He began with pride, believing that all other sins spring from this fountainhead of arrogance. What, after all, was original sin but the sin of pride, a wish to be equal to God?

Christ's life is an illustration of meekness. His incarnation, the *kenosis*, is the emptying of himself by taking the form of a servant and being born in human likeness. Basically, meekness is not self-centered; it is God-centered. It is a humble recognition of human limitations and a confident conviction in divine resources. Meekness implies wise choices commensurate with the will of God. Furthermore, it means the use of the spiritual self to hear the voice of God speaking to our hearts. It is the ability to not conform or comply with current ideologies.

In Christ, we see God in the full glory of his humility. His presence among people was humble-hearted, and at the very end, during the Last Supper, we see the ultimate sign of humility. It was necessary that his disciples know him as God's own Son, so what kind of sign did he choose to give them to remember and emulate? Did he sit on the throne and ask his disciples to bow down before him in homage? No! He took a towel and performed the task of the lowest slave, the task that no one else wished to perform: he washed his disciples' feet.

When Jesus refers to the *kingdom of heaven*, he is referring to now, the present. He reassured his disciples by example that his power came through his Father. A good starting point to utilize this inner power is to be meek, to be humble, and to realize that God is the source of all power. As you become conscious of God's power within you, you no longer need to emphasize who you are. Jesus says, *"Those who want to save their life will lose it, and those who lose their life for my sake will find it"* (Matt 16:25). In essence, he tells us to lose our self that we may find our self. Here, *losing* implies *letting go of the false self*, the self that performs for an audience and conforms to social expectations.

In wishing to feel important, we demand recognition, even if unconsciously, for something we did or said. We seek attention by talking about our accomplishments. We exaggerate events, or we complain about our problems. We want to impress others through our possessions, knowledge, good looks, physical strength, status, and so on. Some individuals insist that they are always right and that others are wrong; they often take criticism personally and feel offended and angry.

We are aware of angry reactions to the cruelty, misery, negativity, selfishness, and violence that exist in our world. If our inner state is subject to any of these evils, we need to take serious responsibility. We can become alert and attentive to our thoughts, for they become feelings, and feelings become words. If we are not sensitive, words may give the wrong idea of who we really are. Why not look within and face our reality? The true self is what the New Testament defines as the *kingdom within*. Everything good, noble, gentle, pleasant, and generous emanates from the true self. Once we remove distortions and superficialities, we are able to see the potential of the true self—not as the world sees us, but as God sees us: his creation, his children.

As Christians we cannot allow ourselves to be dragged down by the tides of political power or to be led by the smell of material profit. The Greek word *praos*, which we translate as "meek," has the connotation "to tame, or to make gentle." It was used in reference to animals, such as a wild horse or dog, or a tiger for the circus. For ourselves, it implies that a university scholar, a theologian, or a scientist becomes a gentle person and shares knowledge and life with humility; that a violent person disciplines him- or herself to behave in a nonviolent way; that a sinner sees the truth about his or her life, repents, and makes a better beginning. Saint Chrysostom, a fourth-century church father, reminds us of our human vulnerability: "The lion can be tamed to be obedient, but your own wrath renders you wilder than that of any lion."

In nature, *tame* implies harnessing for a good purpose that which is wild and unrestrained. Niagara Falls is an example of raw and unrestrained power. Tremendous forces are involved as the Niagara River dashes madly over the cliff. This vast energy was wasted for countless centuries until the human mind conceived the idea of building several large power plants to harness the waterfall for electricity. Today the falls have been *tamed*: the water turns great turbines to generate electricity for many Eastern cities.

"Blessed are the meek" does not mean we must surrender to people, rather, we need to surrender to God with faith. In the Old Testament, God asked Abraham to offer Isaac, his only son as a sacrifice. Abraham was prepared to obey, but as he was about to execute his son, God instantly intervened and rewarded his faith. In the place of Isaac, God gave Abraham a ram to sacrifice. Abraham's faith and meekness were ultimately rewarded when God offered him the Promised Land:

> He leads the humble in what is right,
> and teaches the humble his way.

> All the paths of the LORD are steadfast love and
>   faithfulness,
>   for those who keep his covenant and his decrees.
>   (Ps 25:9–10)

The meek are promised a place to rest their feet and find comfort:

> The meek shall inherit the earth,
>   and rejoice in abundant prosperity. (Ps 37:11)

In the biblical context it means that the meek—those people who are humble and have no high wish of outward glory—will receive all the blessings that God has promised.

In the New Testament, we find the ultimate example of human meekness in Mary's response to the archangel Gabriel: *"Here am I, the servant of the Lord; let it be with me according to your word"* (Luke 1:38). It was Mary's total surrender to and acceptance of God's will that gave flesh to the Second Person of the Holy Trinity. Through her, the Creator of the universe became One of us in the flesh. She gave birth to Jesus, the Savior of the world; she nourished and raised him; she stood by him until his last hour on the earth, as he—once again with utmost humility—accepted death on the cross.

We become aware of Jesus' meekness as we read the gospels. He was born in a stable, a real stable, unlike the colorful nativity scene displayed during the Christmas season. Most likely, the stable in that poor village in Bethlehem was only four rough walls, a dirty floor, a roof of beams and slate. It was dark and reeking; in a clean area, the owner had piled hay and food for the animals. It was not by chance that Christ, the Son of God, was born in a filthy stable. He came to bring forgiveness of sin and joy to the life of people. He came to pave their way toward his kingdom. Unlike the kings of the world who ruled by power, control, and fear, the Son of God offered a kingdom that had no need of armies and weapons. In his kingdom the power exists within each human being. The kingdom that Christ promises is not an ethereal paradise of winged beings at home somewhere in outer space. His kingdom consists of people like us who, although dead, are raised body and soul from death and are in God's joyful presence.

In this beatitude, we see a promise of a land for the meek. In this divine gift of meekness, we can find meaning and purpose in this life, and we sense a prelude to our ultimate bliss in heaven. In Psalm 8:3–6, there is a wonderful tribute to the divine part of man:

> When I look at your heavens, the work of your fingers,
>   the moon and the stars that you have established;
> what are human beings that you are mindful of them,
>   mortals, that you care for them?
>
> Yet, you have made them a little lower than God,
>   and crowned them with glory and honor.
> You have given them dominion over the works of
>   your hands;
>   you have put all things under their feet.

As we meditate on the above verses, we realize God's special care and love for human beings. "For God so loved the world that he gave his only Son, so that everyone who believes in him may not perish but have eternal life" (John 3:16). When we feel weary or discouraged or emotionally hurt, it is his love that comforts and heals us and that gives us the inner energy to be strong and loving.

31

MEDITATION

Our Third Be–attitude

Christ's life is a perfect example of humility. The more we contemplate his exemplary life, the more grateful we become. In humility he made the stable his first home. Today, humbly he enters our hearts, and lets his divine light enlighten our life.

Lord Jesus, protect me from the sin of pride.

Lord our God, I believe that I am a part of your divine plan. You have endowed me with ability and strength to do what needs to be done each day. Grant me the spirit of meekness that I may pursue the purpose that you have for me in this life. Amen.

4

THE HUNGRY

In Christ's time, hunger and thirst were major concerns for the people in Palestine. Even today, hunger continues to affect millions of people. Sadly enough, it exists even in the middle of our affluent society in America. It is not fair to blame the poor and say, "Let them work so they can eat, just like we do."

Blessed are those who hunger and thirst for righteousness,
for they will be filled.

In Victor Hugo's celebrated novel *Les Miserables,* the pivotal event is a desperate man's theft of a loaf of bread in order to prevent his sister's children from starving. The theft costs Jean Valjean nineteen years in prison. When he is released, he cannot find a job or a place to lodge. Finally, a kind bishop offers him food and a place to stay. That night, Jean Valjean steals the bishop's silver and flees from his home. The local police catch him and bring him and the stolen silver back to face the bishop.

The bishop looks at the thief and says, "I'm delighted to see you. Have you forgotten that I gave you the candlesticks as well?" The bishop's reaction surprises the police and causes a sudden transformation in Valjean's heart. He keeps the candlesticks as a symbol of forgiveness and commits to a life of helping others. He becomes a good and honest man, but he cannot find a decent job to make a living. He struggles to survive in a heartless society, which is better organized to punish than to help. The social order is manifested in the austere Inspector Javert, who knows only the law of punishment and who harasses Valjean for twenty years.

As the story unfolds, several kinds of evil surface, but the evil that stands out is the physical hunger of children in a poor and hostile world. The story vividly reveals the author's hunger for a compassionate social order, a society in which no one is driven to steal in order to prevent the starvation of those who are defenseless. Forcefully, Jean Valjean fights against the injustices of his time and moves among his people acting in a Christ-like manner. Victor Hugo portrays this character as an advocate for "spiritual hunger" and for righteousness.

Growing up in the little village of Moria in the Greek island of Mytilene during World War II, I experienced a terrible famine. During the four-year Nazi occupation of the village of Moria, more than three hundred people, out of the town's two thousand inhabitants, died of starvation. I was lucky to survive. Having no fountains, no rivers, and no running water at home, we depended on the community well, from which we were permitted to draw a limited amount of drinking water. I went across deserts and over mountains in search of food. In my journey of eighty-five kilometers, I remember being thirsty for many hours.

For a teenager, enduring long periods of hunger was pitiable—the worst of all miseries. Stealing our fields, animals, and supplies, the Nazis inflicted on us the punishment of gradual starvation. Hunger became a creeping disease, with death ever-imminent. Old and young, children and infants—all were consumed and exhausted by hunger. They lost their color, their skin turned black, their knees buckled, and their eyes lay useless in hollow sockets. Many, with their last breath, begged, crying, "Please, give me just a bite of bread. I'm dying." As I recall the desperate cries, I realize why our Lord used those painful, yet strong words, *Blessed are those who hunger and thirst.* Yet his emphasis is about a different kind of hunger and thirst; it is the hunger and thirst for righteousness. Blessed are the righteous people who want and pursue what is right, like a thirsty person in the desert in search of an oasis.

The word *righteousness* in its original gospel language is *dikaiosyne*, which means "justice"—a state of living a morally correct life, blameless in the eyes of God and neighbors. Simply it means *right thinking.* We can indulge in fuzzy attitudes regarding the concept of righteousness. We can attend church faithfully, holding a Bible or a prayer book, lighting candles, and making generous donations periodically. These are all good actions, but they are a far cry from Jesus' concept of righteousness. An important element of the Christian faith is the condition of the mind, our attitude. An ethically correct mind is the bridge that connects us with God.

At some time in our life, many of us have been treated unjustly. Our first impulse is to retaliate, to strike back, or to find a way to get even. When we see others being mistreated, we are also tempted to defend them or to take revenge on their behalf. It is hard to sit and watch people being taken advantage of—especially if the offenders seem to go unpunished. Rendering justice, punishing the offender, or returning evil for evil is not our job. Christ is the judge. Our part is to treat others fairly and with compassion.

Jesus spoke of attitudes. In essence, he taught us that we have an important responsibility to keep our minds focused on God. At heart, Jesus was a revolutionary. He came to set the world on fire, to change the old order, and to establish the kingdom of righteousness on earth. However, his was a spiritual revolution. He had no desire to overthrow governments. His cause was to change the way people thought, felt, and acted. For Jesus, great numbers were not needed to change the world order. Even as it takes only a pinch of salt to change the taste of a meal, so his handful of chosen, hard-working, and dedicated men changed the consciousness of the world. The twelve apostles were poor, uneducated fishermen who lived a simple life near Lake Tiberias—better known as the Sea of Galilee. They abandoned their fishing gear and followed him.

Without material means, without money, without weapons, and with only faith in our Lord Jesus Christ, the small group of fishermen marched forward into the adverse conditions of a corrupt world. If someone were to ask them where they were going, they would probably have answered: "We are going out among all nations to tell everyone the good news about Christ, the Son of God, who came into our world not to judge but to save us."

Anyone hearing such a response from the mouths of twelve illiterate men would question their sanity. But behind these men lay the power and wisdom of God—God, who became man and walked this earth; Jesus, the God-man who taught the truth about life and right living and who performed miracles among humans and in nature. Eventually, he was crucified for our salvation, he was buried and resurrected, and he ascended into heaven. To continue his work of redemption, his disciples established the Church. They worked hard to continue to bring the Spirit to earth, and sacrificed their lives to propagate God's plan of salvation.

Through the Church and its spiritual leaders, Christ chooses you and me and challenges us to accept the responsibility of bringing his example and teachings to others.

When we are touched by the Spirit of Christ, our own existence suddenly reveals a new dimension. Philosophy, wisdom, scientific knowledge, and all accomplishments are works of the human mind. With a keener insight, we realize that Christ wants us to see God and feel the inherent potential of our gifts. It is this power that enables us to be mindful of the needs of others and to be willing to give whatever is necessary. With the intention of giving, we should not seek to dominate or control another person; rather, our gifts represent God's loving force working through us, making the miracle of love a reality.

This is how Jesus expressed God's love: he moved toward people, healing, comforting, raising the dead, restoring health, delivering people from the power of the devil, and blessing the faithful. His nature was to cry when his friends cried, to laugh when his friends laughed, and to forgive sins so that tears could turn to joy. He treated people with kindness, respect, and generosity. He accepted them with unconditional love, regardless of who they were. For the sinners, he had compassion, and by his example he introduced a correct way of thinking and acting.

To find the right path, we need to have a clear vision, and we need to give up negative thoughts and distorted perceptions. We must be hungry and thirsty to bring a state of righteousness into our present life. Our thirsty souls can be quenched only by the water of life that Jesus offers. "*Let anyone who is thirsty come to me, and let the one who believes in me drink*" (John 7:37–38). Jesus spoke essentially the same words to the Samaritan woman at Jacob's well. Dissatisfied with her life, she was looking for happiness in the wrong place. She had been married five times and was currently living with a man to whom she was not married. Jesus did not say to her, "You are a sinful woman; do not come near me." Instead, he said: *"Everyone who drinks of this water will be thirsty again, but those who drink of the water that I will give them will never be thirsty. The water that I give will become in them a spring of water gushing up to eternal life"* (John 4:13–14). The life that Christ offers is a deep, soul-satisfying contentment that infuses our life with peace and serenity. It is an inner feeling that allows us freedom and energy to express ourselves, to follow our noble dreams despite what resistances we face, and to fall asleep at night without feeling guilty or fretting about what tomorrow will bring.

If we would like to have the lasting joy that Christ offers, we need to be hungry and thirsty for correct thinking and moral values. It takes a radical change of attitude. We need to have a strong desire for a good life, for personal wholeness and righteousness. In this beatitude, Christ teaches us to focus our hunger and thirst not on food and possessions but on a life of unity with God, a life of concern for others, and a life transformed by love.

Years ago, *The New Yorker* published an essay with an intriguing title: "An Inquiry into Enoughness." Today, there is no such thing as *enough* of anything: enough money, enough power, enough accomplishments. Ask the average person you meet what they want out of life. Most people will answer, "All I want is to be happy," but few will define the kind of happiness they want. Some people work hard because they want to buy a house and a car, or they may want better working conditions. These are familiar and normal aspirations.

In my practice of psychotherapy, I often wonder why people with so many reasons to be happy feel so acutely that something is missing in their lives. Could their lives be going in the wrong direction? What about their troubled sons and daughters? Some children of affluent families have only fleeting glimpses of their busy or absent parents and often feel like neglected orphans.

Oscar Wilde once said, "In this world there are only two tragedies: One is not getting what one wants, and the other is getting it." He warns us that no matter how hard we work at being successful, success will not satisfy us. Even the rich, famous, and powerful, whom society applauds, find themselves yearning for something more, because wealth, fame, and power cannot satisfy the hunger of the soul. Unhappiness, and physical and mental illness, often originate from an ailing soul that is ignored. We need to take care of our soul, the spiritual dimension of self. Just as our bodies need food and water, our souls need God in our lives.

MEDITATION

Our Fourth Be-attitude

Every time we are treated unjustly, rather than reacting with revenge, think of our Lord and the injustices he suffered. He never took revenge. He even forgave those who crucified him. He is a God of love and justice. Injustice may triumph but only for a while. Eventually it is defeated. As our soul thirsts for justice, we become aware that part of our human nature is divine.

Lord Jesus, I want to be a just person.

Lord my God, you are my hope, my strength, and my salvation. Instill in me a life of righteousness. Lead my thoughts and actions on the right path. Satisfy the hunger and thirst of my soul with your presence in my life. Amen.

5

THE MERCIFUL

Mercy is a kind and compassionate gesture of giving something good to someone who is in need. It is not a superficial expression of sympathy. The mercy that the Lord praises is not a big donation of money or material possessions. It is rather the gift of our time and talent to our neighbor. It does not have to be a spectacular action. What is important is the gift of ourselves and the degree of love we invest in our deeds. Taking a meal to a sick neighbor, working with a charitable group, or supporting an abandoned orphan in a war-torn country—each of these can be considered an act of mercy.

Blessed are the merciful, for they will receive mercy.

In our times, the word *mercy* is often used in a judicial context—a reporter might note: "The defendant threw himself on the mercy of the court." A clement judge, taking into consideration the particular circumstances of the crime, may decide not to punish a guilty person with the full severity of the law. He might reduce the sentence to less time in prison.

In the Acts of the Apostles, one of Peter's miracles is an example of the kind of mercy praised by the Lord:

And a man lame from birth was being carried in. People would lay him daily at the gate of the tem-

ple called the Beautiful Gate so that he could ask
for alms from those entering the temple. When he
saw Peter and John about to go into the temple, he
asked them for alms. Peter looked intently at him,
as did John, and said, "Look at us." And he fixed
his attention on them, expecting to receive something from them. But Peter said, "I have no silver
or gold, but what I have I give you; in the name of
Jesus Christ of Nazareth, stand up and walk."
And he took him by the right hand and raised him
up; and immediately his feet and ankles were
made strong. Jumping up, he stood and began to
walk, and he entered the temple with them, walking and leaping and praising God. (Acts 3:2–8)

Saint Peter's expression of mercy was to appropriate the
power that Jesus had given him and use it to empower the
lame man. A similar gesture of mercy occurs when we make
ourselves available to comfort a troubled person. Our presence can be comforting to those who are ill or who suffer
from emotional pain.

The Hebrew word for mercy connotes graciousness,
kindness, self-giving, tenderness, or unconditional love. In
the Old Testament, the word *mercy* is used as an attribute of
God or an appeal for God's help: *"Have mercy on me, O
God, according to your steadfast love; according to your
abundant mercy blot out my transgressions"* (Ps 51:1).

In the Greek New Testament, the word for mercy that
is used in this beatitude is *eleos*. We hear this word in the
chanting of both Orthodox and Catholic liturgies: *Kyrie elei-
son*—"Lord, have mercy." From the word *eleos*, we derive
the word *eleimosyne*—gracious deeds done for those in need;
merciful giving; almsgiving. Jesus warned the scribes and

Pharisees of the woe they were bringing upon themselves by concentrating on details of religious observance while they *"neglected the weightier matters of the law: justice and mercy and faith"* (Matt 23:23).

In the parable of the Good Samaritan, the Lord's claim for mercy comes across vividly:

A man who knows the Law and has never broken it raises the question, *"Who is my neighbor?"* In answer, Christ tells the story of the traveler who is attacked and wounded by thieves. His life is in danger and he is saved, not by the two fellow Jews who passed by and crossed over to the other side of the road, but by a nonbeliever, an outsider, a Samaritan. Christ asks which of these three men was a neighbor to the man who was beaten by thieves? The man of the law replied, *"'The one who showed him mercy.' Jesus said to him, 'Go and do likewise.'"* (Luke 10:29–37).

Mercy is an intrinsic attribute of God. The life of Jesus is replete with examples of mercy made manifest through his actions and personality.

When a person looks at people in the way a loving father looks after his children and is willing to endure their failures and shortcomings, then that person behaves in a Christ-like manner—God in action. People of faith perceive wrongdoers as God's children, each having a soul. The morally weak, the physically decrepit, the mentally impaired, the spiritually ignorant—all need merciful help and understanding.

Mercy is an essential part of our call to the Christian life. Each time we recite the Lord's Prayer, we say: *"And forgive us our debts as we forgive our debtors."* Forgiveness and mercy are synonymous. Sometimes we want mercy for ourselves but resist extending it to others. We are eager to judge, or to see only one side of a situation. We may be decent people with good intentions, but we are also human. In vulnerable moments, we may say or behave in a manner devoid of mercy. It is then that we hear the voice of Christ calling us to show mercy, living and thinking of God's mercy toward us.

In every encounter with another person, we have an instant reaction and often an instant judgment. In reality, we are not defining the other person: we are defining ourselves. Perhaps we have difficulty in accepting our own insecurities and negative feelings about who we really are. Consequently, we may project these failings onto another human being. Is that fair to the other person? Even if we do not approve of another person's behavior, is it our right to be critical?

When an intimate friend or a spouse makes mistakes, let's not be eager to judge or to lecture. Rather, respond with a sense of respect and compassion. Remind yourself that we all make mistakes along the way. Any judgment, regardless of how polite and gentle it may be, is a covert attempt on our part to upgrade ourselves by comparison. If we judge our brothers or sisters, and in our thoughts place them in an inferior category, are we really better than they are? As we look around, not with judgmental eyes, but with loving eyes, we realize that all people are human, all are creatures of God. They, too, have an immortal soul. Instead of judging others and making negative pronouncements about them, we can take a profound look into our inner self. Simply examine and evaluate constructively our own life. At times the fear of being destitute, ill, dysfunctional, homeless, or abused causes us to judge persons in such situations critically. Whether self-imposed, the result of an addiction, or a circumstance of life—the suffering of others represents a spiritual deficit within our human community. We can improve that deficit with thoughts of love and compassion instead of arrogant criticism. The Christian life requires that we show compassion. As we focus on the good in another, it becomes easier to act with compassion. We may not necessarily make world-shaking contributions, but we can each do something within our means with sensitivity, awareness, and love. Start today, if only in a small way, and reach out to help someone who needs help.

Listen to the words of Saint Teresa of Avila:

> Christ has no physical body now on earth but yours, no hands but yours, no feet but yours; you are the eyes through which Christ's compassion must look out on the world; yours are the feet with which he is to go about doing good; yours are the hands with which he is to bless men and women now.

There is much pain in the world—whether from poverty, oppression, pollution, cruelty, disease, or war—it is our current reality. Our world is in desperate need of healing.

As we practice mercy—kindness, love, and compassion for others—we move closer to God. Being closer to God, we discover our true selves; the selves we are meant to be; the selves that God created—the merciful power within us.

A false self desires honor, power, and superiority over the true self and thrives on glory and praise. It exaggerates experiences, wants to climb the corporate ladder, appears clever, attends special parties, knows the best restaurants, and chooses the best wines. How real is a person with such attitude?

In the quest of the true self, we begin to appreciate and accept the life that God calls us to have. We do not really know ourselves. We know only our habits and the personality we assume each day. We come to realize that we do not really know our inner depth, our spiritual potential. We can attain three levels of this self–knowledge: outer, inner, deep.

1. To know our outer self is to know the self and the mask we show to the world; this outer self displays our surface emotions, extravagant lifestyle, habits, and personality. This is the self visible to everyone, sometimes admired, at other times envied.
2. Our inner self is visible only to ourselves and selected, intimate others. However, to know it well requires that we consciously look inward. Our secret hopes, fears, and fantasies live here, hidden from most others and partly kept hidden from ourselves.
3. Our deep self is our true self: the image and like-ness of God. This image and likeness convey an important truth about our spiritual identity. The image is our permanent potential for commu-nion with God; the likeness is the actual result of God's grace and power within each of us.

Self-knowledge is the path to our soul. Saint Augustine prayed, "Let me know myself, Lord, and I shall know You." We learn to know God as the more loving parts of us are nat-urally magnified, and the more sinful parts are gradually fading. In other words, God desires for us to be the persons we were created to be—to be simply and purely ourselves— and to love God. It is a double journey: coming closer to God means becoming instruments of his mercy, and finding our true selves means discovering the divine power within that enables us to be merciful.

In spite of the unnecessary suffering in the world, con-cern and compassion seem to grow. Individuals, religious groups, and charitable institutions seem to expand—beyond government systems and political powers—to embrace the concept of mercy for the welfare of all people.

Mother Teresa's Missionaries of Charity offer dramatic examples of sacrificial giving and the joy it produces. The sisters have an austere lifestyle. They leave the comforts of home and live among the poorest of the poor. At their central house in Calcutta, they are packed three or four to a room; their only personal possessions are two dresses and a bucket for washing. They eat food similar to that of the poor, and despite the suffocating Indian heat, they have no air conditioning. They rise before dawn and spend their days working in the slums. It is an existence that most of us would regard as difficult, if not downright depressing. Yet when a television interviewer visited Mother Teresa, he exclaimed:

"The thing I notice about you and the hundreds of sisters who now form your team is that you all look so happy! Is it a put-on?"

"Oh no," she replied, "not at all. Nothing makes you happier than when you really reach out in mercy to someone who is badly hurt."

"I swear," wrote the interviewer afterward, "that I have never experienced so sharp a realization of the meaning of joy."

Einstein expressed the way to happiness as only a genius could:

A human being is a part of the whole called by us "Universe," a part limited in time and space. He experiences himself, his thoughts and feelings as something separated from the rest, a kind of optical delusion of his consciousness. This delusion is a kind of prison for us, restricting us to our personal desires and to affection for a few persons nearest to us. Our task must be to free ourselves from this prison by widening our circle of compassion to embrace all living creatures and the whole of nature in its beauty.

Our Lord's admonition to be *merciful* is a command that each of us can remember daily in every expression of life. Yet being merciful is a matter of attitude. Simply, if we want to be loved and accepted, we must love and accept others. If we want to have friends, we must behave in a friendly manner. If we want others to treat us justly, we must treat others justly. We may not always be able to change the world around us, but we can change our thoughts about the world. When we do that, we change our world, which is the world of our perceptions.

This may be a hard lesson for many of us. Our tendency is to think, "If I had only gone to college"…"If my spouse would only listen to me"…"If my boss would only give me a break"… "If I had only bought my own home"…"If I only lived in a warmer climate"…"If only this or that would happen, *then* I would be happy." Such thinking stifles our growth because it negates the present and thinks of a future that is only a fantasy.

Attitudes and reactions are attracting forces. In other words, we mentally invite our own conditions by our thoughts. When we think of failing—"Well, I don't think I am going to have any luck in the effort"—we fulfill our prophecy, and we fail. We program our failure.

We can change the pattern of attraction and change the world. As long as we have an enemy, we also have enmity. We may debate whether or not the enemy caused the enmity or the enmity drew the enemy. If we want freedom enough to take the first step, we need to neutralize the mental pattern of enmity within ourselves. When we have no enmity, we have no enemies, as far as we are concerned.

Often, through a sense of insufficiency as a person, we form our attitudes after we have appraised our world. As a result we say, "I don't know what's wrong with me; nobody wants to be my friend; I don't think anybody likes me; people are staring at me, so I am self-conscious; some of my associates seem to be slighting me and that hurts me." Or, "They say we are in for an economic recession, so I'm worried; there is danger before me, so I'm afraid." These are negative thoughts, and they result in a completely unrealistic approach to life.

When we decide the kind of world we want to experience, the kind of friends we want to have, the success we want to achieve, and the kind of conditions we would like to see manifested in our home, our neighborhood, and our society, then we begin to access the irresistible power that God makes available to us.

The wonderful corollary to this type of thinking is that when we build an attitude of love, mercy, justice, friendliness, and peace, we no longer look for or identify with any apparent enmity or injustice in others. We will attract the best kind of people and draw the very best from all the people with whom we associate. It can be done.

MEDITATION

Our Fifth Be–attitude

Through God's mercy, we sense love in our hearts that transforms our attitude toward ourselves and particularly our relationships. God's love and mercy encompass unconditional acceptance, compassion, forgiveness, hope, reconciliation, and peace. As we apply these qualities, we find true happiness and attain a higher spiritual level.

Lord Jesus Christ, have mercy on me.

Lord, extend your loving mercy to all. You have given us wisdom and the power of thought to show mercy and kindness to those in need. Help us focus our thoughts upon only those things that are of benefit to the soul and contribute to our inner peace. Amen.

6

THE PURE IN HEART

We read in Saint John's Gospel, "*No one has ever seen God*" (John 1:18). Yet, Jesus promises, "*Blessed are the pure in heart, for they will see God*" (Matt 5:8). This seems contradictory. Of course, purity of heart as referred to by Jesus depends on the guidance of our actions by wisdom. Thoughts, attitudes, and actions need to be enriched by the qualities of the soul: conscience, forgiveness, love, mercy, service, and self-control. Purity of the intellect gives one the power of correct reasoning, but purity of heart connects us with God.

Blessed are the pure in heart, for they will see God.

The *American Heritage Dictionary*, besides identifying the heart as a muscle, offers a nonphysical definition: it is a vital center of one's being, aspirations, emotions, and sensibilities; the repository of one's deepest desires and sincerest feeling and beliefs. Metaphorically, the heart encapsulates the wholeness of the human being, including our spiritual dimension, our soul. Focus your thoughts on the good, the true, and the beautiful, and then you will see God. When we are distracted by negative thoughts, it is hard to see anything good and positive. We hear voices that tell us, "If you are stressed, have a drink, go to a shrink and unload your problems, take medicine, turn on the television and relax." You and I know that these "quick fixes" are not the real answer.

There are times when we relax and free our minds from earthly cares, past mistakes, and worries. It is then that we see God's creation in its full glory: the birth and growth of a child, the beauty and color of nature, the wonder of the animal kingdom. Each of God's creatures is designed with utter perfection; it is with profound gratitude we can repeat the words of the Psalmist: "*How many are your works, O* LORD! *In wisdom you have made them all*" (Ps 104:24).

Any attachment can take over our life if we are not aware that it consumes our time and energy. For example, attachment to accomplishments, ambitions, wealth, status, or possessions leads to dependency on them, and we may forget who we are. It is normal to want beautiful things, but when we are obsessed by them, we detach ourselves emotionally from others and live a life of isolation. We think we can be happy with exterior attachments, but inevitably we are disappointed because no external attachment can satisfy the inner self.

As we let go of jealousy, judgment, negativity, pride, and any other weakness, we allow God's power to work within us. Sensing God's presence is achieved by making our spiritual life the first priority. This includes developing our integrity and character and not seeking just short-lived pleasures. The issue in this particular beatitude is about purifying the heart that we may see God; it is not simply about seeking satisfaction.

In the story *The Little Prince*, Antoine de Saint-Exupéry speaks of the importance of the heart. It is only with the heart that one can see rightly; what is essential is invisible to the eye. A pure heart is free of possessiveness; it is capable of mourning; and it hungers and thirsts for what is right, merciful, and loving. A pure heart is free of vices, anger, greed, jealousy, hostility, and vengeance. It is a heart that thirsts for what is right; it is a loving and generous heart.

In the Old Testament, purity implies rituals—ceremonial washings to keep the body clean, and discipline rituals dictating what foods may or may not be eaten. Besides a physical condition, purity implies an inner quality: wholeness or integrity of spirit; a person free from sin.

In the New Testament, Christ stresses the purity of the heart. He says those who follow the laws of purity and lack mercy *"are like whitewashed tombs, which on the outside look beautiful, but inside they are full of the bones of the dead and of all kinds of filth"* (Matt 23:27).

When the prophet Nathan made King David realize that he had committed two grave sins—adultery and murder—David cried: *"Create in me a clean heart, O God, and put a new and right spirit within me"* (Ps 51:10). When King David looked inward, what did he find in his heart? Power, lust, hardness of heart, coldness of heart, and a desire to do whatever felt good for his own flesh. Acknowledging his crimes, he turned to God with a penitent mind and a humble heart and said:

> Have mercy on me, O God,
>   according to your steadfast love;
> according to your abundant mercy
>   blot out my transgressions.
> Wash me thoroughly from my iniquity,
>   and cleanse me from my sin.
> For I know my transgressions,
>   and my sin is ever before me.
> Against you, you alone, have I sinned,
>   and done what is evil in your sight,

> so that you are justified in your sentence
> and blameless when you pass judgment. (Ps 51:1–4)

The purer the heart, the more aware it is of the Creator's presence in its life. A pure heart is endlessly seeking a more God-centered life, and that is accomplished by a simple, ongoing, spontaneous prayer. Coming or going, sitting or standing, working or resting, in church or at home, a brief prayer can always be on our lips: *Lord Jesus Christ, Son of God, have mercy upon me.* This pleading sentence, known as the *Jesus Prayer*, has helped many people through the ages to move from the thinking mind to the feeling heart. This simple prayer will give us inner contentment, peace, and sobriety; it connects us instantly with our Lord.

The seventh-century Saint Isaac of Syria asks:

What is purity? It is a heart full of compassion for the whole created nature…And what is a compassionate heart? It is a heart that burns for all creation, for the birds, for the beasts, for the devils, for every creature. When he thinks about them, when he looks at them, his eyes fill with tears. So strong, so violent is his compassion…that his heart breaks when he sees pain and suffering of the humblest creature. That is why he prays with tears at every moment…for all the enemies of truth and for all who cause him harm, that they may be protected and forgiven. He prays ever for serpents in the boundless compassion that wells up in his heart after God's likeness.

God's likeness suggests that we think, feel, and act in a godly way by making a concerted effort to keep our mind clean. It is with the mind that we see, and it is with the mind that we perceive. If the mind is clear, we see clearly. If the mind is darkened by negativity or confused by distorted thinking, vision suffers. Caught in a cloud of smoke, the eyes become teary and painful, allowing no visibility. If the mind is inundated with fantasies, delusions, and incorrect ideas, there can be no peace, no vision.

Many people think that living a godly life will cause them to miss out on fun. They find it hard to believe that a life of fullness, joy, and abundance is the result of being obedient to the teachings of Christ. Christian living is the most dynamic, creative, and meaningful force in the world. People who were in love or who are in love at present understand the intensity and power of the experience. It is a state of meaningful and satisfying existence. It is meaningful because someone needs us, wants us, loves us, and makes us feel special. By the same token, we need and want the companionship of another; we want someone who cares and loves and makes us feel special. When we are together we feel complete. The feeling can become so intense that the rest of the world becomes insignificant.

Christ's invitation to be pure in heart means to live in a right relationship with God. Developing a deep understanding of God causes us to enjoy life fully and also gives us a deeper understanding of people. The secret of a balanced and enjoyable life is to live so that it is easy for our Lord to reveal himself through the power of the Holy Spirit working in us. This is the true road to a rewarding life.

We are capable of attaining spiritual greatness but we need models that can inspire us. Where are they? They are not often found in front of a television set, in a bar, or within pages of celebrity magazines. God says, through Saint Paul, *"Therefore come out from them, and be separate from them,...and touch nothing unclean; then I will welcome you, and I will be your father, and you shall be my sons and daughters*" (2 Cor 6:17–18).

We live in a technological age that puts its faith in the perfection of the computer and other electronic devices. Human beings tend to become like the god they worship; fortunately as people of faith, our agony does not allow us to become like robots. Trusting God's plan for our life, we can counterbalance the sterility of the perfect machine. We have the choice to return to the Scriptures and documents of dedicated people who gave form and shape to the Christian faith.

With a receptive mind, respect, and faith in the Creator, we will rediscover the good sources that nurture the soul. Saint Isaac the Syrian said, "Faith that God will act is essential." And Jesus said, "*As you have believed, let it be done unto you*" (Matt 8:13). It is an experience of grace that happens to those who are simple of heart and fervent in hope. Simplicity means, among other things, to avoid trying to explain or analyze what you feel about God in purely intellectual terms.

As we think of Christ's sacrifice, we come face to face with the greatest act of compassion and love that the world has ever known: the Son of God took our guilt upon himself and sacrificed his life so that we could be redeemed from sin. His grace and love continue for each one of us. Even though we are forgetful and often drift away from God, Christ waits patiently and lovingly for us to turn back to him. We can be grateful for his abundant compassion and repeat the words of Saint Paul, "*But by the grace of God I am what I am, and his grace toward me has not been in vain. On the contrary, I worked harder than any of them—though it was not I, but the grace of God that is with me*" (1 Cor 15:10).

Questioned about what makes a person unclean, the Lord answered, "*What comes out of the mouth proceeds from the heart, and this is what defiles"* (Matt 15:18). Saint Paul clarifies the meaning of this:

> Finally, beloved, whatever is true, whatever is honorable, whatever is just, whatever is pure, whatever is pleasing, whatever is commendable, if there is any excellence and if there is anything worthy of praise, think about these things. Keep on doing the things that you have learned and received and heard and seen in me, and the God of peace will be with you. (Phil 4:8–9)

It is impossible to have a clean heart if we are victims of our passions. Bad morality weakens the character and allows evil thoughts to defile the inner part of the self. This can be seen at the family level when spouses lose respect for each other or victimize their children by being indifferent or permissive. As a result, the whole family is in danger of falling apart.

It may not be within our own individual power to overcome evil or to set the world right, but we can see the world rightly. Seeing it rightly means that we leave behind illusions and move toward a godly life. If we want to change the world or be an influence for such a change, we must begin within ourselves by changing the way we perceive it. We should not dwell only on the evil and the things that are wrong, for evil attracts more evil.

Now, we cannot always control what happens to us, but we can control what we think—and our perception of life at any particular moment. Even if we cannot shape our life the way we want, we must at least try as hard as we can to not degrade it. Why not view life from the highest rather than the lowest vantage point? Christ sees the totality of a human being. He sees the divine potential in each of us, the ability to be positive, creative, and loving. He associated with all classes of people, exemplifying a human-divine life, a *how to be* attitude. He wants us to be like him: "*For I have set you an example, that you also should do as I have done*" (John 13:15). He tells us we are special: "*You are my friends....I do not call you servants any longer*" (John 15:14–15). When people recognize their own potential—God's power within—they begin to have a foretaste of heaven on earth.

MEDITATION

Our Sixth Be–attitude

To attain a pure heart is a challenge for anyone of faith who responds to the voice of the soul. It is a process of refining thoughts and observing actions lest we make wrong choices. Within us are the riches of heaven. The kingdom of heaven is within you, said the Lord. Outside of you is death, and the door to death is sin. Enter within yourself and remain in your heart, for there you will find God.

Lord Jesus, establish in me a pure heart.

Lord, let me see the world not as it is, but as you see it. Show me the way to purify my heart that I may be worthy of your presence in my daily life. It is only with my heart that I can see what may be invisible to my eyes. Amen.

7

THE PEACEMAKERS

Christ's wisdom about a happy life and his understanding of the human condition can banish conflicts and the horror of war and bring peace. Being made in the image and likeness of God—endowed with godly qualities—we can captivate human hearts with the power of love. We must, or humanity will surely perish. If leaders of nations have power to declare war against each other, they also have the power and ability to negotiate and make peace.

Blessed are the peacemakers, for they will be called children of God.

We are spiritual beings with the potential for peace and harmony within ourselves. We are capable of becoming models of godly behavior, radiating the spirit of Christ. The moment we believe and call ourselves children of God, we take on the task of becoming peacemakers.

This is the miracle of this beatitude. As we realize that we are children of God, the world around us gradually changes in a dramatic way. We see things more clearly, the light is turned on, and darkness disappears. It is as simple as that—but it takes effort. Many of the external aspects of life that previously were so important and meaningful seem insignificant. Our need to be special and different diminishes, and we are more easily satisfied. It is our spiritual self, our soul, where peace is born, blossoms, and develops.

If we truly want to be peacemakers, we need to develop our own inner peace. We cannot bring peace to anyone if we do not feel peaceful within. However, to acquire peace of mind and soul, we may have to move to an entirely different level of life. Obsessing about our external life—what our body looks like, what others think of us, what others have that we do not have, how much money we are making, how we impress others—makes us restless, anxious, and unhappy. We will enjoy greater peace of mind when we are not focusing on what's wrong with our life, but when we are paying attention to what's right in our life and then proceed to strengthen it. Remember, the world won't change, but our perception of it will, especially when we notice there are people around us who are caring, loving, and supportive. Of course, all of us want financial freedom, the right relationship, the right job, the right church, and comfortable living conditions. Most of us yearn for a good time, fun, entertainment, intimacy, sexual fulfillment, power, and material possessions. As important as these may appear, they do not allow much time to connect with the inner self to see what is really significant for our peace of mind.

The word *peace* in the Greek language is *eirene*. It describes God's ultimate blessing—a joyful state of being and contentment. It was the gift that he offered and continues to offer to his followers. He had no earthly estate, no inheritance to leave to his disciples: "*Foxes have holes, and the birds of the air have nests; but the Son of Man has nowhere to lay his head*" (Luke 9:58). But he gave them what they needed most—divine peace.

Christ instructed his disciples that, upon entering a dwelling, their first action should be a blessing: "*Peace to this house*" (Luke 10:5). Peace was a prerequisite for their mission, for their daily life, and for their eventual salvation.

At the Last Supper, before Jesus was led off to be crucified, he said to his disciples: *"Peace I leave with you; my peace I give to you. I do not give to you as the world gives. Do not let your hearts be troubled, and do not let them be afraid"* (John 14:27). After his resurrection, when the disciples were hiding behind locked doors, afraid of the enemies of their Master, Jesus came and stood among them and said, *"Peace be with you"* (John 20:19). Christ offers his peace to each one of us, because he wants us to be happy: *"I speak these things in the world so that they may have my joy made complete in themselves"* (John 17:13).

Saint Paul realized the need for inner peace. When he wrote letters to the young churches of Asia, Greece, and Rome, he often began with a blessing of peace: *"Grace and peace to you from God our Father and the Lord Jesus Christ."* The gift of peace is not a principle or social ideal but is the gift of Christ himself. When Christ is present in our life, we have peace. He enters our world to reassure us that we are sons and daughters of God. What he is by nature, we become by grace. Through his church, he continues to teach us that we are God's children, members of his kingdom.

Christ said, *"Blessed are the peacemakers,"* which implies an active role. We cannot simply be quiet recipients, expecting others to make peace with us or bring peace into our lives. If we cherish the peace that Christ promises, we need an attitude of reconciliation between self and others, making amends wherever there is conflict. Those who help establish God's peace—providing care to those in need, helping two neighbors reconcile, or restoring unity within a family—assist in God's activity in our world. God may not have physical hands to reach out and embrace those who need comfort, but he assigns the task of love to you and me. A peacemaker is doing what God intends, and bringing peace

60

into our interactions with others indicates that we are his children. An old Chinese proverb states this realization of peace in the world simply:

> If there be righteousness in the heart, there will be
>   beauty in the character.
> If there is beauty in the character, there will be
>   harmony in the home.
> If there is harmony in the home, there will be order in
>   the nation.
> When there is order in the nation, there will be peace
>   in the world.

Periodically I hear the cry of some of my clients, especially from those who seem to have problems in their relationships: "All I want is some peace in my life." As I listen to these words, I hear myself forty years ago, while I was studying for my doctoral degree. My supervisor, an insightful psychologist, reacted to my wish with insight that has never left me. With raised eyebrows, she said, "Peter, you are young and naive. There is no peace in this world. There never was, and there never will be. As long as we inhabit human bodies, we will live a life combating good and evil. Stress and tension are unavoidable because of our choices." She paused for a second, perused the faces of her audience and with a gentle smile, said, "Peace only exists in one place, in the cemetery."

"In the cemetery?" I asked.

"You are of Greek origin. You should know what the word means."

"*Kemeterion*," I said, "a place where people are asleep."

"Well, that's where a person finds peace," she said. "In real life, eventually we wake up and have to face reality: making a living, combating the odds that come our way, seeking comfort, and establishing ourselves socially. Life is an ongoing struggle."

I found the thought disturbing, that peace exists only in the cemetery. Yet, it is a profound statement. The peace we are looking for in this world, either in our pursuit of material wealth or in a simple struggle for survival, is finally realized in the cemetery where wealth, fame, and glory have no value.

Contemporary technology, cultural conformity, science, and mass media assault our senses with noise, color, stimulation, and ceaseless advertising about *things* that we need. We do our daily work for financial survival, on the weekends we race off in different directions to buy *things*, possibly the latest gadget to make our life easier, or we go out to eat, to play, or to seek pleasure. The noise of modern life makes it hard to hear ourselves think. Cell phones and endless e-mails keep us in constant contact with others. Television invades our living rooms with other people's lives, current tragedies, soap operas, commercials, artificial worlds, and graphic images, leaving little time to process and test our own thoughts. Where are the moments of peace?

All the rushing around cannot help us escape from that deep, often-unrecognized need within ourselves to feel peace. If we do not have inner peace, how can we feel peaceful in the presence of others? For inner harmony and contentment, we need to be in good standing with God, in thoughts, feelings, and actions.

Our soul thrives on quiet time, inner peace, and prayer, the only true fountain of spiritual nourishment. To connect with our soul and rekindle our spirit, we have to rid ourselves of all the obstacles that come between our actions and the purity of thought. It would be beneficial to give ourselves a few minutes of quiet time during each day, preferably in the morning. Find a place to be totally alone. Initially, set aside ten minutes and gradually increase the time. Shut down the inner dialogue—no thoughts—and make a new path toward peace.

Losing sight of what the reality of life is or what our priorities are, many of us hide behind the noise, unwilling to face ourselves and the truth about who we really are. Once we accept our own reality, we can move forward bravely and with confidence, make wise choices, and cherish the results of these choices. Of course, we can explore life, listen to others, read books, and weigh opinions, but eventually we have to make our own decisions, following direction from within ourselves.

Surely conflicts, pain, quarrels, troubles, and wars are a part of life, but there is peace. We believe that we have an immortal soul abiding in a physical body and living in our present world. To some extent we experience peace, especially during our prayers, worship services, spiritual readings, or in peaceful places where we enjoy nature's glory. These are precious quiet hours that we all desire and appreciate until the cellular phone rings: "Your daughter was in a car accident and the ambulance is taking her to the nearest hospital"..."The bank called to say they cannot give you a second home-equity loan"..."Next month your position at work will be discontinued"..."Your car insurance has been canceled because you owe two monthly payments—they say they warned you last month." Suddenly, the little peace we experienced is replaced by a surge of frustration. We try to find a rational answer, but there is none. These things do happen and they challenge our faith. No attack or defense or justification changes an event. How we react to tragedy, pain, and difficult times depends upon the depth of our faith in God. But we still want peace.

Christ promises a different kind of peace, not an improved version of the world, nor a ceasing of war, nor a resolution of conflicts. His peace is paradoxical: *"Do not think that I have come to bring peace to the earth; I have not come to bring peace, but a sword"* (Matt 10:34). Pious Jews regarded Jesus as a disturber of the peace. They felt that he ignored their traditions by healing people on the Sabbath, resurrecting the dead, and cleansing the Temple in Jerusalem from the merchants and moneychangers. His teachings were a stumbling block to the status quo.

When Jesus spoke of peace, he meant peace as an inner condition, which is not attained without our own intense effort. Our part is to reconcile ourselves with others and harmonize our life with our surroundings in order to attain the peace that Christ promised: *"Peace I leave with you; my peace I give to you. I do not give the peace that the world gives."* The peace that the world gives is a result of compromises, a combination of self-interests and ambition to accumulate wealth. This type of peace promises material goods, happiness, and elixirs that last only for a little while, for they cultivate a hunger for more and more, leaving the soul ever thirsty, empty, and restless.

The disciples, having witnessed the horror of the crucifixion, had serious doubts about who Jesus really was. They were afraid they would be persecuted as well and have to suffer the same lot because they were his followers. So, they needed peace. His peace surpasses our human understanding, and it comes to us as we attune our life to God's will, using the talents he has given us to do something good and beneficial for others.

The lack of peace in our life occurs when we make statements like the following:

64

- I cannot have peace unless things change.
- I'm angry because nothing good happens in my life.
- Everybody else seems to have all the luck. I don't know why it doesn't come my way.
- I cannot forgive myself for dropping out of college just to get married.
- My daughter is approaching forty and she's not married yet. I won't have any peace until I see her married.

Furthermore, unconscious or even conscious thoughts that we direct toward others can prevent us from having peace. The following are a few examples:

- My mother gives me no peace; she interferes with everything in my life; I'll never have any peace until I move miles away.
- I cannot be at peace with my husband. He is demanding and always wants me to attend to him on hand and foot. He needs to grow up.
- When my brother is around, I cannot be at peace. Something he did to me when I was a child is still hurting.

All our assumptions or thoughts that remain unexamined and unresolved tend to convince us that we cannot be at peace. Unrealistic expectations confuse the reality of our potential. "*With Christ in me, I can do all things,*" claims Saint Paul (Phil 4:13). God's power within enables us to have compassion, to forgive, to let go, and to have a better understanding of the human condition.

Developing a sense of inner peace implies that we are willing to see our small hypocrisies and large illusions, and

65

that we are learning to be forthright and honest with ourselves and with others. We regain peace when we see with clarity the true nature of things. Our friend, our spouse, or our boss is who he or she is. No one can be like us, nor can we change and conform to a different lifestyle, hoping someone will like us more. If we want to have a joyful and peaceful spirit, we can listen to Saint Paul's admonition:

> Do not worry about anything, but in everything by prayer and supplication with thanksgiving let your requests be made known to God. And the peace of God, which surpasses all understanding, will guard your hearts and your minds in Christ Jesus. (Phil 4:6–7)

Complete peace of mind and heart are God's gifts to us; but this peace is not given without our own intense effort. God will give us anything for the benefit of life when we work with all our strength and pray with all our heart and mind to attain it.

MEDITATION

Our Seventh Be–attitude

Tired and frustrated by what this world offers, our soul craves peace. Peace is so precious that God himself came to earth to establish peace among people *"Come to me, all you that are weary and are carrying heavy burdens, and I will give you rest"* (Matt 11:28). By his mission of love, reconciliation, and his ultimate sacrifice, Christ became the Prince of Peace.

Lord Jesus, instill peace in my heart.

The Peacemakers

Lord our God, we are grateful that you have accepted us as your children, in spite of who we are. Help us to purify our hearts that we may be worthy to be called your children, and to rediscover the peace that you promise. Let your peace that surpasses our human understanding fill our hearts and minds. Amen.

8

THE PERSECUTED

Life presents us with many challenges. The challenges become stronger when we are living a life of righteousness. When we think and act justly, following faithfully the teachings of our Lord—loving, forgiving, being compassionate and generous—we definitely face disturbing opposition. Saint Paul relates his experiences that came about because of his faith, his love, and his steadfastness: *"What persecutions I have endured! Yet the Lord rescued me from all of them. Indeed, all who want to live a godly life in Christ Jesus will be persecuted"* (2 Tim 3:11–12).

Under such circumstances, we need to be strong in our convictions about God's presence in our life. We must make a decision. Are we going to subject ourselves to the void of contemporary vogue that promises happiness but causes anxiety, or are we going to choose a godly life that gives inner peace and promises us the kingdom of heaven?

Blessed are those who are persecuted for righteousness' sake, for theirs is the kingdom of heaven.

The blessings of each beatitude do not simply mean being happy as we follow Christ's teachings, but also being empowered to be part of God's kingdom. Christ places in each of us the ability we need to discover this kingdom within. As we believe the truth about ourselves, the strength within us is released, and we realize that God's abundance, peace, and power are within us. We lack for nothing.

It takes courage and determination to safeguard and protect our life from predators. This beatitude affirms the truth that in time of adversity, when we are vehemently attacked by external forces or inner resistance, God never leaves us. He gives us the needed strength and comfort to endure frustration or pain.

The Lord never promised to keep us free from all adversity or to adjust all circumstances for our benefit and pleasure. But his words confirm the divine power within us. They imply that we need to have courage so we can transcend any form of trouble as he did. He endured crucifixion and death, but rose from the dead. We, too, will rise from any sort of suffering.

Jesus Christ, God in human form, gave us a portrait of real life. It is not the Garden of Eden, a state of bliss. It is an eventful and exciting journey with periodic, unpleasant interruptions. Unexpected obstacles appear along the way, disrupt our peace, and interfere with our good intentions. Subtle opposition causes spiritual inertia, bringing a halt to our efforts to perform worthwhile activities. Whether these forces are internal or external, they cause impasses, pain, and physical and emotional deterioration.

A youngster who is ridiculed by his peers because he will not join them in smoking marijuana is emotionally persecuted for righteousness' sake. A woman is pursued by her unscrupulous married employer; she avoids his advances and refuses his invitation to a candlelit dinner. Suddenly, her position in the company is terminated, and she is dismissed. She is persecuted for righteousness' sake. Both the youngster and the woman chose to follow the right path and not act in ways that would bring shame into their life. As a result, they had to face adversity.

At least we can be grateful that we do have some good teachers, mentors, and spiritual counselors who offer a healthy direction and alternative. Above all, in the middle of this, our Lord is present to sustain us and guide us through the most difficult adversity. The person who experiences trouble feels pain; at times the pain is great—perhaps it is not an outer, visible pain but rather an inner, emotional, mental, or spiritual hurt. Saint Paul's description of his experience reveals some principles about adversity that we can apply when we face anguish or feel persecuted:

> Pray for deliverance and find comfort in God's presence.
> Recognize we are not alone in our adversity.
> Rely on God's power as sufficient to carry us through troubled times.

When adversity hits us, as it surely will at some point in life, we are wise to say: No matter what I may experience, regardless of my pain, the Lord is with me. He is walking with me through this troublesome time. He is by my side. He is aware of my condition and knows the way through the situation to a brighter and better tomorrow. His grace is sufficient for me.

In many cases, the explanation for our adversity or the cause of our persecution may be something that is totally beyond our control and influence. The experience of illness or the death of a loved one, the loss of property from a hurricane, a financial loss in the stock market, the breakup of a marriage—each of these painful events is a form of persecution. As we listen to the words that our Lord said to Paul, *"My grace is sufficient for you, for power is made perfect in weakness*" (2 Cor 12:9), we become aware that the Lord may not instantly remove our problem, but he will compensate fully for it. In whatever ways we are weak, he will make us strong. He will fill the crevices of our pain, lack of ability, heartache, and discouragement with his presence. What we cannot do, he will do. Jesus Christ is the Healer, the only One who can heal body, soul, and spirit. His treatment is gentle. The results are wonderful.

How reassuring is Saint Paul's message to the Romans:

> We know that all things work together for good for those who love God, who are called according to his purpose....Who will separate us from the love of Christ? Will hardship, or distress, or persecution, or famine, or nakedness, or peril, or sword? As it is written, "For your sake we are being killed all day long; we are accounted as sheep to be slaughtered." No, in all these things we are more than conquerors through him who loved us. For I am convinced that neither death, nor life, nor angels, nor rulers, nor things present, nor things to come, nor powers, nor height, nor depth, nor anything else in all creation, will be able to separate us from the love of God in Christ Jesus our Lord. (Rom 8:28, 35–39)

If problems are not a result of our choices, they definitely have a hidden purpose. We may have an answer some day, especially as our understanding of God's promise, "*for theirs is the kingdom of heaven*," becomes an undisputed conviction and we will begin to feel the healing power of the Holy Spirit. The best way to this is to trust God for an answer that will bring you to a place of peace in your heart and mind.

This beatitude deals with our thinking. The persecution takes place within our mind, and the persecutor is an errant thought in our own mind. As we set a course of righteousness or right thinking, or when we begin a program of discipline and self-restraint, we invariably run into the crosscurrents of our own thoughts. We resist our own potential of having a better and healthier life. We become the enemy of our own happiness.

We may know a hard-hearted, arrogant, obnoxious person who turns against us, badmouths us, and has reasons for ignoring us. There was a time when this person was a friend but now behaves like an enemy for no reason of which we are aware. The Lord tells us how to treat such an individual: *"Love your enemies, pray for those who persecute you"* (Matt 5:44).

Saint Paul describes for us the attitude of a person who truly lives in the presence of God. He is not afraid to include even those who persecute us, who have bad things to say about us, who take pleasure in pulling us down:

> Bless those who persecute you; bless and do not curse them. Rejoice with those who rejoice, weep with those who weep. Live in harmony with one another; do not be haughty, but associate with the lowly; do not claim to be wiser than you are. Do not repay anyone evil for evil, but take thought for what is noble in the sight of all. If it is possible, so far as it depends on you, live peaceably with all. (Rom 12:14–21)

Saint Paul anticipates and emphasizes the availability of good people who practice Christ's love and who are willing to go to the limits of their being.

In physics, to move an object that is at rest or to stop an object that is in motion, we must overcome inertia. The inertial force maintains an object at rest or in motion unless it is acted upon by an external force. There is a kind of mental inertia that resists change. Even the effort to improve our life necessitates our coming to grips with the states of mind that have directed the kind of life we are now experiencing. Saint Paul undoubtedly was puzzled over his mental inertia when he said:

> For I do not do the good I want, but the evil I do not want is what I do. For I delight in the law of God in my inmost self, but I see in my members another law at war with the law of my mind, bringing me into captivity. (Rom 7:19, 22, 23)

The adversity Saint Paul encountered in his lifetime is summarized in four words, *thorn in the flesh*. The thorn he describes is not the small garden variety. He endured painful persecutions and beatings whenever he attempted to preach the gospel of Jesus Christ, but his story left us with valuable lessons. For Paul, the thorn was *"a messenger of Satan to torment me"* (2 Cor 12:7). In the Greek language, there is one word that may be translated as either *torment* or *beat*; it is used in Mark 14:65 to describe the ordeal that Jesus endured: *"The guards also took him over and beat him."* Through his experience with a thorn in the flesh, Saint Paul discovered that God's power reached its peak at the lowest point of his adversity. He wrote, *"Therefore, I take pleasure in infirmities, in reproaches, in needs, in persecutions, in distress, for Christ's sake. For when I am weak, then I am strong* (2 Cor 12:10). Saint Paul learned through the experience that when he allowed the grace of the Lord to be sufficient in his weakness, he was actually stronger as a result.

What the Lord did for Saint Paul, he will also do for you and me when we experience personal adversity that threatens to destroy us. He will raise us up by his power.

When we are struck with pain, we are often amazed at how many other people have experienced the same pain—pain to which in the past we may have been blind. Couples who feel secure and happy in their marriages may not have much sympathy or empathy with divorced couples. But when their marriage disintegrates, they have much greater compassion for those who also face the possibility of divorce. The same goes for those with sickness. The person who has the most compassion for someone diagnosed with terminal illness is likely to be a person who currently has, or has conquered, that same sickness.

The fact of the matter is that we rarely have great empathy or sympathy for the suffering of others unless our lives have been touched by the same or similar problems. Adversity either hardens or softens us. If we let it harden us, we are subject to more adversity. If we allow it to soften us, adversity can lead us to advance in our understanding of and compassion for others.

There are many lessons to be learned as we go through hard times. We can discover the power within. Even if your human nature is pulling and keeping you down, the divine part that exists within you is pulling you up. It is a sign of your growth, an awakening of your soul.

You are blessed because the persecution represents the first reaction to the external force, which is of divine origin *"for the one who is in you is greater than the one who is in the world"* (1 John 4:4). In other words, you are on the way, and inward persecution of the warring thoughts may prove it. Press on past the inertial pull of your humanity to release your divinity.

74

Connect with the spiritual dimension of yourself and taste true salvation that includes fulfillment, joy, peace, and life in all its fullness. You are to be who God wants you to be; you are to feel within you the good that has no opposite and the joy of being human with divine qualities. In the presence of God, you feel free from fear, from persecution, and from suffering. You become complete.

When Jesus said to Zacchaeus, "*I must stay at your house today,*" instant transformation took place. Realizing his sinfulness, Zacchaeus repenting, said:

"Look, half of my possessions, Lord, I will give to the poor; and if I have defrauded anyone of anything, I will pay back four times as much." Then Jesus said to him, "Today salvation has come to this house, because he too is a son of Abraham. For the Son of Man came to seek out and to save the lost." (Luke 19:5–10)

Truly, this is a great and most important attitude that can be attained today, not tomorrow or in the future. Jesus emphasizes the importance of *today*. When we pray, "*Give us this day our daily bread,*" we do not necessarily mean bread or food for the body. Our physical needs are important. On a deeper level, we are asking God to give food for the soul. The word *epiousion*—"what is of essence"—implies spiritual food. The bread for the soul is God's divine word, the Christian teachings.

When our life gets disrupted as conflict, dissatisfaction, or emotional or even physical violence arises against our being, it is not bread that we need, but *what is of essence for our life*, for our spiritual sustenance. Only God can provide what is of essence. Seek out the challenge that provides a good attitude.

MEDITATION

Our Eighth Be–attitude

We become aware of God's presence in our life as we
recall how people saw and experienced Christ's presence. He
was gentle, kind, and compassionate; to the sick and suffering, he was a healer; to the sinner, he was forgiving; to the
crowds who came to hear him, he was the fountain of wisdom and a friend, spreading joy and peace.

Lord Jesus, be present in my life.

Lord, in my quest for truth, grant me a deepening
awareness and an increasing release of my inner spiritual
potential. My being is not just bones, flesh, and blood. There
is a deeper part of me that sustains me. Lord, help me to
remain connected with my spiritual nature. Amen.

9

THE REVILED

The kingdom of heaven is the newness of a life that starts here and continues after death. The Jews did not want to hear about such a kingdom; they wanted a kingdom on earth. So they looked for a reason to overpower Jesus and eventually do away with him. Possibly there might be another, *mightier* messiah for them, they thought, a king who would liberate them from their misery.

Jesus knew this all along, but he continued to preach the gospel of love and righteousness, the *good news* of salvation. His exemplary life—his compassion to forgive sinners, feed the hungry, heal the sick, and resurrect the dead—disturbed the leaders of the Temple. Jesus challenged their hypocrisy and, knowing the destiny of his followers who were to continue his ministry, he made them aware of the dangers ahead.

Blessed are you when people revile you and persecute you and utter all kinds of evil against you falsely.

This beatitude speaks of God's unconditional and protective love. He extends his encompassing blessing to all those who are insulted, persecuted, and slandered. Jesus Christ was opposed from the very beginning. When Mary and Joseph brought the infant Jesus to the Temple, Simeon, a righteous and devout man, took him into his arms and said to the mother: *"This child is destined for the falling and the rising of many in Israel, and to be a sign that will be opposed"* (Luke 2:34).

Joseph and Mary had to take Jesus to Egypt to escape Herod's edict to kill every male child in and around Bethlehem who were two years old and younger. When Jesus began his ministry, his own people did not accept him. They expected a mighty king to rescue them from the Roman yoke and establish an earthly kingdom for them. But *this* king, God in human flesh, spoke of a heavenly kingdom.

As his disciples diligently performed their work spreading the good news of salvation, they faced all kinds of trouble—false accusations, imprisonment, persecution, stoning, and death. Saint Paul gives a brief account of what happened to him among his own people. Because he spoke of Christ and his love for the whole world, he endured imprisonments, floggings, and was often near death.

> Five times I have received from the Jews the forty lashes minus one. Three times I was beaten with rods. Once I received a stoning. Three times I was shipwrecked; for a night and a day I was adrift at sea; on frequent journeys, in danger from rivers, danger from bandits, danger from my own people, danger from Gentiles, danger in the city, danger in the wilderness, danger at sea, danger from false brothers and sisters; in toil and hardship, through many a sleepless night, hungry and thirsty, often without food, cold and naked. And, besides other things, I am under daily pressure because of my anxiety for all the churches. (2 Cor 11:23–29)

God is not separate from the trials of humanity; he is not a mere spectator. God is participating in our life and not just tolerating human suffering or healing the pain. God participates in it with us and through Christ, who has suffered with us. God may allow adversity or persecution but not beyond our human endurance. He provides the strength to endure the trials until they come to an end. When all our tears are over, we will look back at them and smile, not in derision but in joy. We do a little of that now. After a great worry is lifted, a great problem is solved, a great sickness is over, a great pain is relieved, it looks very different. Today's troubles are just that—today's troubles. A season of trouble—accusations, harassment, pain, and persecution—is a season of trouble; ultimately the season passes and something good will come of it. This is what gives life both meaning and hope. We have a caring and loving God on our side.

Evil is the result of the need to control and dominate others. It lies in selfish interests, political power, manipulation, exploitation, or greed. Another aspect of evil, mainly beyond our control, is nature's unexpected catastrophes—floods, earthquakes, and hurricanes. The familiar question is asked: What does God do about this sort of thing?

While God surely tolerates evil, it appears that, beyond tolerating it, God is even making use of it and *"gives life to the dead and calls into existence the things that do not exist"* (Rom 4:17). Maybe this is the great work of transformation.

To our endless "why's" about human suffering, God's answer is "Jesus Christ." God never promised to keep us from adversity or to adjust all circumstances for our exclusive benefit and pleasure. Problems, needs, and troubles plague all humanity. No one is immune to them. However, we can count on the Lord being with us in times of adversity, calamity, tragedy, hardship, and pain. The most wonderful and amazing event in human history is that God became a man. John the Evangelist begins his first letter with the following words: *"We declare to you what was from the beginning, what we have heard, what we have seen with our eyes, what we have looked at and touched with our hands"* (1 John 1:1).

The incarnation of Christ was the most comforting contribution to human suffering. Christ came to save each one of us from corruption and death. In one of his surviving homilies, John Chrysostom compares the condition of society to a harlot.

> God does not bring her to heaven. He comes down to earth in human form....He finds her thick with sores and oppressed by devils. She is scared and flees away. He calls her, saying, "Why are you afraid? I am not a judge, but a physician. I came not to judge the world, but save the world."

Chrysostom's metaphor speaks to our hearts today. God does not hesitate to enter our suffering world. Like a lover, he seeks to be present in and intimate with our lives in spite of our condition. When we are undergoing a most painful experience, we can take a look at the cross and hear our Lord's agonizing cry. *"My God, my God, why have you forsaken me?"* This is something that *"no eye has seen, nor ear heard, nor the human heart conceived"* (1 Cor 2:9). The immortal and omnipotent God of life allowed the power of evil to destroy him on the cross. God's answer to the problem of suffering did not happen only 2,000 years ago, but continues to happen in our time. All our suffering becomes Christ's suffering, and it is his way of working our salvation and granting us eternal joy. The cross explains the possibility of our pain.

As we apply the teachings of Christ in our life, we may meet material-minded people who do not appreciate our per-

spective. It is important not to be dismayed or intimidated by
them. They may avoid us or not include us in their company.
They may label and categorize us negatively. We may
momentarily be tempted to retaliate, but those moments will
pass and we will not feel affected. When Christ says *"I am
with you always"* (Matt 28:20), he means that he will protect
us and give us strength. Mentally and physically we sense his
divine presence in prayer. In his company we feel blessed.

It takes faith in his miraculous birth, exemplary life,
painful crucifixion, and glorious resurrection. *"Behold I
stand at the door and knock; if anyone... opens the door I
will come in and eat with him"* (Rev 3:20). Our part is to
open the door of our heart, receive his message, and apply
his teachings in all our experiences throughout our lives.
Christ's invitation for us to follow him implies that we may
have to go through our own "personal Good Friday." An
ancient hymn from the Greek Orthodox liturgy for Holy
Week speaks of Christ's invitation:

> We are going to Jerusalem; and the Son of man
> will be delivered up as it is written of Him. Come,
> then, minds purified, let us walk with Him, and
> for His sake, die to the delights of this life; that we
> may also live with Him, and hear him declare:
> "No longer do I go to Jerusalem to suffer; but I go
> up to my Father, who is your Father, my God and
> your God. And I will raise you up with me to the
> upper Jerusalem, to the Kingdom of Heaven."

Christ's presence on earth was not just limited to his
public ministry, a three-year effort to save the world. It was,
and it is, an eternal companionship because of his infinite
love. Far from a sentimental love, his is a true love that
includes the cross. It is comforting that Christ walks beside

us in the lowest places of our lives. When we are in pain, he is pain with us; when we grieve our losses, he grieves with us; when we are rejected or despised, he is rejected and despised. In our darkest time, he brings us light; in our fear of death, he promises resurrection. As he died and rose again from the dead, he gave new meaning to our death.

The thought of death seeps slowly into our daily life. The physical self ages and loses vitality. Our youth, health, strength, hopes, dreams, children, and our lives—all dribble away like water through our fingers. Not even our best efforts can hold our lives together. Lest we be tempted and succumb to despair, God provides strength and ways to escape from our trials and tribulations. We hear his voice through the words of Saint Paul who says:

> No testing has overtaken you that is not common to everyone. God is faithful, and he will not let you be tested beyond your strength, but with the testing he will also provide the way out so that you may be able to endure it. (1 Cor 10:13)

God's love for humanity is evident in the three areas of Christ's ministry. First, he came among the people: he suffered; he wept. Second, in becoming man, he transformed the meaning of our suffering: it is now part of his work of redemption that the Church continues. Third, he died and rose: our ultimate resurrection makes a difference to the world. The belief that God will bring us back to life is his promise. To confirm this promise, God died on the cross, but he also rose from the dead. There is no greater hope than the hope of resurrection. Saint Paul says, "*If Christ has not been raised, then our proclamation has been in vain and your faith has been in vain.... If for this life only we have hoped in Christ, we are of all people most to be pitied*" (1 Cor 15:14, 19).

Believing that God will bring us back to life offers the difference between eternal death and eternal joy in his kingdom. The reality of our resurrection echoes Christ's appearance on earth. The following is a prophecy dating back to sometime between the years 100 and 80 BC:

> The LORD sets the prisoners free;
> the LORD opens the eyes of the blind.
> The LORD lifts up those who are bowed down;
> the LORD loves the righteous.
> The LORD watches over the strangers;
> he upholds the orphan and the widow,
> but the way of the wicked he brings to ruin.
>   (Ps 146:7–9)

These statements give us hope in Christ the Lord and in his resurrection, which is offered to every believer.

Why are so many people atheists or agnostics? Because, although on one level they believe, on another level they do not accept. Like Ivan Karamazov in *The Brothers Karamazov* by Fyodor Dostoevsky, they are either doubters or rebels. Perhaps they are angry because God does not answer their endless why's: Why do joints stiffen as we get older? Why do good intentions or sensible plans go nonsensically off course? Why do innocent children suffer? Why are there genetic defects in newborn children? Why do so many die before they have had a chance to live? If God is good, why is there so much ugliness in the world? These questions have no answer and are a source of disbelief.

When the disciples announced to the apostle Thomas that Christ had risen from the dead—"*We have seen the Lord*"—he doubted them:

"Unless I see the mark of the nails in his hands, and put my finger in the mark of the nails and my hand in his side, I will not believe."

A week later, [Jesus'] disciples were again in the house, and Thomas was with them. Although the door was shut, Jesus came and stood among them....Then he said to Thomas, "Put your finger here and see my hands. Reach out your hand and put it in my side. Do not doubt but believe." Thomas answered him, "My Lord and my God!" Jesus said to him, "Have you believed because you have seen me? Blessed are those who have not seen and yet have come to believe." (John 20:25–29)

To doubt is human; to believe is divine.

Logic requires proof; the heart requires faith. When logic reaches an impasse, faith takes over. When we struggle to reconcile a good God with a seemingly evil world, we will never be able to find satisfactory answers. One problem is that we have a hard time accepting that God is God and that we are human. We would like to be God and be in total control of life and death. That's not the case. We are human, and there will be a time when we will doubt. Doubt is a sign that we are growing and pursuing the truth about God and ourselves. Perhaps it is easier to belong to a group than to belong to God. To belong to a group, one is convinced the group is "right," and we comply with its rules, thinking they serve a purpose; but to belong to God, one always knows one can be wrong like anybody else. They are two different journeys, and the choice is ours.

When the current of life is against us, we do not need to fight it. Our Lord God is ever-present. We are still under his grace and are still blessed. Persecution represents the *external force*; however, "*the one who is in you is greater than the one who is in the world*" (1 John 4:4). Jesus Christ helped others in spite of intense persecution; kept God's laws and commandments in spite of great temptation; in the darkest hours of anguish said, "*Thy will be done*"—he is our example. We can trust in God, and God will empower us. Our lives have a purpose far beyond comfort, ease, or pleasure—to become like his Son, Jesus Christ.

MEDITATION

Our Ninth Be-attitude

Our daily reality is a society inundated by conflicts. Arrogance, greed, mistrust, suspicion, and selfishness surround us and weaken our faith. Conflict is not necessarily external. It exists within us, causing anger and doubt. In sorrow, you are our Comforter; in danger, you are our Protector; in sickness, you are our Healer, and in oppression, you are our Savior.

Lord Jesus, you are my only source of comfort.

Lord, Master of my life, in times of trouble and doubt give me the courage to endure any adversity. Help my disbelief, protect me, and show me the way to follow you. Amen.

10

REJOICE AND BE GLAD!

The Beatitudes end with Jesus' gift to all human beings—the gift of joy. As we contemplate the deeper meaning of the Beatitudes, we sense inner contentment in spite of life's challenges and opposing forces.

Rejoice and be glad, for your reward is great in heaven.

The Christian faith centers on the joy in Christ and his resurrection. What does this mean? Once we recognize and follow the will of God and develop an attitude of love and righteousness, we no longer experience temporary happiness, but the inner feeling of lasting joy. The Lord clarifies that feeling when he says,

> "As the Father has loved me, so I have loved you; abide in my love. If you keep my commandments, you will abide in my love, just as I have kept my Father's commandments and abide in his love. I have said these things to you so that my joy may be in you, and that your joy may be complete." (John 15:9–11)

In spite of life's adversities, joy is the element that every Christian heart needs to attain. In reality, however, we often search for joy in the wrong places, mainly in worldly possessions. Saint Paul grounds us firmly when he says:

> Rejoice in the Lord always; again I will say, Rejoice. Let your gentleness be known to everyone. The Lord is near. Do not worry about anything, but in everything by prayer and supplication with thanksgiving let your requests be made known to God. And the peace of God, which surpasses all understanding, will guard your hearts and your minds in Christ Jesus. (Phil 4:4–7)

God created a universe of unimaginable wisdom and perfection. As a master artist, he adorned his creation with spectacular beauty, striking colors, superb tastes, and unsurpassed forms and shapes. All creation, from a minute blade of grass to trees and flowers and the stars, serves a purpose and leaves us in awe. Did God do all this for himself?

We read in the opening of the Bible that once God made the world, plants, and animals, he created Adam and Eve. Our hearts are filled with gratitude when we read the biblical description of the creation of the universe by his word— *"Then God said, 'Let there be light'; and there was light."* God created human beings with loving care and special intimacy by his own hands, molding them out of earth—*"Let us make humankind in our image, according to our likeness"*— and placed them in Paradise, a garden in Eden. We can sense his infinite love. He wanted humans to be happy. Adam and Eve failed to respect the magnitude of Paradise. They disobeyed God's command and they lost God's gift of happiness. We do not need to go back so far; we know what happens in our own life when we make wrong choices or violate rules. We suffer the consequences.

How many *happy* people do you know? I mean individuals who appear, think, feel, and communicate with genuine joy? Granted that many people, surrounded by wealth and luxury, brag and talk about their material accumulations—the big house they moved into, or the summer resort that they just bought last month, the expensive car, the exotic trip they plan to take—and give the impression they are happy. Perhaps they are, and one can wish them well. Of course, things that we buy and own, things that put us seemingly higher on the ladder of success, surely give us temporary happiness. Even people who indulge in alcohol, drugs, illicit sex, crooked deals, and other evil works experience a superficial and perverted satisfaction. But is there a lasting joy within these individuals? All that glitters is not necessarily gold. Appearances can be deceiving and it depends on how we perceive and experience the world around us. While most people would like to be happy, the approach to happiness is different for every individual. We may be endowed with the wisdom of Solomon and have the resourcefulness and intelligence of Odysseus, yet many of us are unable to live a life of contentment.

Some people spend a lifetime, sacrificing their own health and even that of their families to become rich. We can admire them, assuming that they are happy. Yet how do we know that the rich, famous, and successful are really happy? Regardless of the enormous amount of material accumulations and money they acquire, they may still want more. The hunger for more of everything is never satisfied. The idea of *enough* is nonexistent. Some of them may be anxious that something may go wrong, resulting in the loss of everything they own. It's interesting to note that some very wealthy people, knowing they have more than enough, go after glory and fame. One may wonder if glory really provides or guarantees happiness. History records the experience of Xerxes, King of Persia. When he invaded Greece with fifty thousand soldiers, he looked at his surroundings and felt depressed that, fifty years from then, he would not be around to cherish his conquests. Perhaps it was then that the ancient Greeks gave origin to the often-quoted axiom: *"Count no man happy till he dies, free of pain at last."*

Sometimes simplicity provides the basis for a happy life. Pre-Christian history refers to great minds that found happiness by living a simple life. Today we might perceive them as humorous or weird. When the philosopher Socrates, for example, saw a pile of gold and jewelry being borne in procession through the streets of Athens, he exclaimed, *"Look how many things there are that I don't want."* And another example of contentment: As Alexander the Great was passing though Corinth, he saw Diogenes, dressed in rags and sunning himself. The most powerful man of his time asked the philosopher, *"Is there anything that I can do for you?"* Diogenes replied, *"Yes, step out of the way. You are blocking the sun."* Alexander's guards were horrified and steeled themselves for the inevitable outburst from their commander's familiar anger. But he only laughed and remarked, *"If I were not Alexander, I would certainly like to be Diogenes."*

At the birth of the Christian era, there emerged a group of individuals, most of them bearded and wearing simple apparel, who were singularly free of desire for success and wealth. They lived a simple life and were involved in good works and philanthropy. They were the disciples—the bearers of good news of their time. They set out to evangelize the world, telling people about Christ and his teachings of love, compassion, forgiveness, salvation, and suffering. Today, we have missionaries who travel to bring this same Christ to the furthest parts of the world. Organizations in our own country engage in worthwhile projects to secure good education for the young, and they support scientists who continue their research work for medical advancements. All these active and willing people experience a great deal of happiness from their philanthropic endeavors.

In rethinking the part simplicity plays as a component of happiness, I recall my teen years. I was seventeen when one day I decided to travel on foot for six hours to a remote village on the island where I grew up. The purpose of my visit was to find a record, a rare piece of music that a man had in his possession. After asking several people, I was able to track down the man. He was pruning trees in an olive grove. The man responded politely, "My name is Dimitri. Could you wait a half hour? I will finish this work, then take you to my home and give you the record." I did wait, and after an hour's journey through an olive grove, we arrived at his house.

It was a modest hut—one large room where he and his wife lived. In one corner, I saw a wood-burning fire and a cooking pot above the flame. "Sophia, we have a guest with us," Dimitri said jovially. After a few words of introduction and a hearty welcome, Sophia stretched a tablecloth on the floor and placed on it three napkins, spoons, and three slices of homemade bread. She asked us to sit, but there were no chairs. Her husband sat crossed-legged on the floor, and he asked me to sit next to him. Food was served in one big dish; swimming in olive oil were boiled beans garnished with small pieces of ripe tomatoes. Dimitri said grace, and silently we ate from the same plate. When the meal was over, the wife picked up the dish and the utensils from the table cloth and put them on the stone sink.

Dimitri looked at me and said, "Peter, I believe you are too far from home. It's dark outside. Not safe to travel alone at night. Stay over. Tomorrow, go back." I thanked him for his concern. I glanced furtively around the room. *Where in the world am I going to sleep*? I wondered. *There's only one room.* His wife was washing the dishes and spoons in the stone sink. He picked a huge mattress from a corner and unrolled it on the floor. Then he unfolded two thick hand-woven blankets. The sleeping arrangements covered nearly the entire floor. He smiled and said, "Room for everybody."

Sophia turned, and looking around the room said, "While I'll be facing the wall, you boys undress. When you get under the covers, turn your faces and look in the other direction." Dimitri followed the order, and pointed that I should lie on his left side. We both turned, not looking at her. Soon after, Sophia got ready and slid under the blankets, next to her husband. Simultaneously, they said "Goodnight." I replied, "Goodnight, and thank you for your kindness." I had tears in my eyes, not knowing whether I should smile or be sad for them. They had so little, and yet they shared whatever was available to them, including their bed. So here we were, three people sleeping on the floor on the same mattress, with the husband in the middle, the wife on his right, and the stranger on the left. The morning breakfast was mountain tea, a slice of bread, sliced tomatoes, and cured olives. It was a luscious breakfast, served with smiles. As Dimitri was about to leave for work, he gave me the record and wished me a safe trip back home.

Now, more than sixty years later, my experience with Dimitri and Sophia remains vividly in my mind. In subsequent years, when I established my home in the United States, I told that story to my children. Since each one of them had an individual room, they could hardly believe it. Yet it happened to me, and it taught me a great lesson about the virtue of simplicity, which is truly an integral part of happiness.

Maturity is another step necessary for a life of contentment. When we passively sit around and commiserate that life is dreadful and does not meet our expectations—thus feeding our dissatisfactions—it is a sign of immaturity. As we become active and respond responsibly to life's demands without the excuses of *ifs* and *buts*, then we have attained a state of maturity that increases and provides fulfillment and joy.

Another resource for happiness is relationships. A good relationship provides an atmosphere where joy can germinate and blossom. Reciprocal communication, acceptance, sensitivity, respect, symmetrical give-and-take, responsible decision making, and loving interaction—all these qualities cultivate happiness. The tendency to bond closely with another person, acting for the welfare of another as well as for ourselves, is deeply rooted in human nature. Granted that when we act lovingly toward others or show generosity and availability, our ulterior motive may be selfish: the bottom line is that we want others to accept us and love us. This is not a bad thing; it is good selfishness. But when we are self-absorbed and everything we do is totally for ourselves, this is bad selfishness, and needs to be avoided. Although we are all selfish to some degree, we can still move on with life and living, being lovable while loving others. Individuals who lack loving ties with others seem to suffer from poor health and have a greater vulnerability to stress and a higher level of unhappiness.

After his resurrection, Christ appeared to the women and said, "*Do not be afraid*" (Matt 28:10). When he appeared to men, he said, "*Peace be with you*" (Luke 24:36). The path toward peace, joy, and happiness begins the moment you take the next step. Pause for a few minutes and reflect on these attitudes for living. Do you think you can make them part of your life?

MEDITATION

Our Tenth Be-attitude

God wants us to enjoy life. He wants us to think, feel, and do whatever is good and of lasting joy. Jesus calls us each day to do what benefits body and soul that we may have abundant joy. To experience this inner feeling of joy, we need to simplify our life and let the Lord provide the answers.

Lord Jesus, you are my hope and my salvation.

Lord, I am tired of being in mental turmoil. Nothing in my present life seems to relieve me. Grant me the peace and joy you promised to your followers. Instill in me the desire to do what is right in your eyes. You are my hope. I place my trust in you. Amen.

EPILOGUE

While writing this book, an unexpected opportunity presented itself to my wife, Pat, and me—a trip to the Holy Land. As we visited the places where Jesus lived, we visualized him as the Good Shepherd, opening his arms, embracing the world, rejecting no one, and, with unconditional love, inviting everyone to follow him and his example. Passing along the narrow streets of Old Jerusalem, we could envision Jesus comforting the afflicted, healing the sick, breaking bread with poor and rich alike, and forgiving sinners. His life was marked by the miracles he performed, the stories he told, and the message of God's kingdom that he promised. He emphasized that people should not live by bread alone, but must be nourished with spiritual food.

Something unforgettable happened to us while visiting the Garden of Gethsemane. It was noontime and we felt hungry. We sat on a marble bench to rest. Pat had brought two sandwiches for our lunch. It seemed awkward that only she and I would be eating. What about Father Makarios, the Greek monk who was our guide? What about the three other men that sat across from us? Between embarrassment and hesitation, Pat offered one sandwich to Father Makarios. He took it gracefully and began to cut it into four pieces. The sandwich seemed to expand and was cut into four big pieces. In silence, Pat and I looked at each other and smiled; though in disbelief, we were positive the sandwich had grown to feed the four men. Weeks later, in a note reminiscing about the lovely time we spent together,

Father Makarios sent a photo of our small group seated on the marble bench. On the back he wrote, "*We all ate and were satisfied by the grace of Mrs. Pat Kalellis.*" He had seen it, too! We all knew we were fed by the grace of the Holy Spirit.

As we climbed to the top of the hill, where Jesus delivered the sermon that contains the Beatitudes, I felt excited and moved. Joyfully, I began to read the text in the original Greek. I could see Jesus sitting at the peak of nature's amphitheater surrounded by hundreds of people listening to him. Here was the God-man, *Theanthropos*, beautifully fashioned, full of integrity, meek, fiery, and insistent—accepting everyone and promising the ultimate reward, eternal life in God's kingdom. His appearance on earth and his presence in our life signifies a beginning, the birth of a new hope for each of us.

Overwhelmed by the stresses and strains of everyday life, many people desperately seek peace. The key to gaining balance between the society in which we live and our personal interests is to appreciate what is good and beneficial in our life, without becoming trapped by our desires or attached to our possessions, our image, our status, or our ambitions. If we want to be accepted and loved, we need to accept ourselves, accept others, and be loving and lovable.

The totality of our life cannot be reduced to a few isolated frames, any more than a scrapbook of clippings or a photograph album can reflect a whole life. There is a flow to our existence. Some of us are knocked about more than others, striking rock bottom more often than riding the crest. There is a patterned integrity to life—chemical, physical, emotional, and spiritual—and for each of us, that pattern is unique. Each of us is a minute cosmos representing God's creation.

God's Power Within You

In other words, the final reality is that it all begins and ends with the individual's attitude toward life. We cannot delegate others to solve our personal problems any more than we can appoint surrogate breathers. It is our life; we alone are accountable for it. Only we can harvest the yield and determine its richness.

Certainly, there are circumstances and conditions beyond our immediate control, but not nearly as many as we think. In some cases, they may not be the obstacles they appear to be, but rather opportunities. No matter what we think of ourselves, no matter what we have done in our life or with it, no matter how limited our experience seems to be, we are of divine origin. Like the prodigal son, we may have been living off in the far country and have now come to our senses. Now is the time to wake up and realize the depth of our own divine potential, God's power within.

Many Christians comprehend immortality in terms of time. It has often been thought of as a matter of the future located in a place called heaven—another life, a future existence after we die. However, the great truth that Christ teaches is that we do not have to die to be immortal. We are immortal right now. Christ opened the gates of heaven and promised immortality, which is beyond time. We all live in immortality, for Christ is among us.

On Easter morning, millions of people throughout the Christian world proclaim the words, *Christ is risen! Truly he is risen!* Everyone who believes in the risen Lord acknowledges the deep implications of Easter and of this statement, and all Christians build their faith on this acceptance. Dwelling on that first Easter in the right spirit, we will find that the stones of human limitations are rolled away. We no longer see barriers of prejudice or class distinctions; we are no longer hampered by the animosity between nations or

96

minds. We are able to glimpse the divine dimension of ourselves and that same divine part in other people.

God invites us to go deeper rather than to be content with surface matters. Superficiality is the curse of our times. Instant satisfaction, idle talk, and shallow thinking tire out the most tolerant person. What our soul yearns for and needs is profound awareness of the presence of Christ. The Holy Spirit within you will help you in the process, from weakness to strength, from confusion to clarity, from fear to faith, and from sin to holiness.

A Christian attitude can embrace the aim to become more intimately acquainted with Christ. This does not mean that we have to be scholars in theology, nor do we have to become missionaries. Our goal in life is to become intimately acquainted with Christ. *"Strive first for the kingdom of God and his righteousness, and all these things will be given to you as well"* (Matt 6:33).

With Christ as our companion, faith and a Christian attitude will give meaning and purpose to our life. He instills strength and motivation in our work and at home, empowering us to act on the basis of our better moral impulses and values and helping us to be more creative, compassionate, and socially responsible. A Christian attitude reassures us that we are not slaves or victims of a negative social system. We are sons and daughters of God, sharing his glory as co-creators, destined to inherit his eternal kingdom.

No matter who we are, we all experience ups and downs throughout life. Of course we would like our life to be wonderful all the time, but that is not going to happen. Such an attitude may sound pessimistic, but it is realistic. Christ's declaration *"You will know the truth, and the truth will make you free"* (John 8:32) implies that it does not really matter what happens *to* us or *around* us. All that really matters is what happens *within* us—the thoughts and feelings that formulate our attitude. The time is ripe for us to embrace the attitude of the Beatitudes and become people of the Spirit. With a Christian attitude we are drawn closer to God and eventually are partakers of his kingdom.

BIBLIOGRAPHY

The following books have enriched and inspired the writing of *God's Power Within You*:

Agio, Alkistis. *You Can Realize Your Dream*. Westwood, NJ: Cosmos Publishing, 2001.

Butterworth, Eric. *Discover the Power Within You*. New York: Harper & Row, 1968.

Forest, Jim. *The Ladder of the Beatitudes*. Maryknoll, NY: Orbis Books, 2002.

Conley, Benjamin. *The Spiritual Connection: Values, Faith, and Psychotherapy*. Fort Lauderdale, FL: Anthos Publishing, 2001.

Kalellis, Peter M. *Five Steps to Spiritual Growth, A Journey*. Mahwah, NJ: Paulist Press, 2005.

———. *Pick Up Your Couch and Walk: How to Take Back Control of Your Life*. New York: Crossroad, 1998.

Koumoundouros, Nikiphoros. *Stones for Spiritual Construction*. Greece: Phoenix Publishing, 1996.

Rohr, Richard. *Job and the Mystery of Suffering: Spiritual Reflections*. New York: Crossroad, 2002.

Stanley, Charles. *The Source of My Strength*. Nashville, TN: Thomas Nelson, 1994.

———. *Living The Extraordinary Life*. Nashville, TN: Thomas Nelson, 2005.

Papakosta, Seraphim. *The Sermon on the Mount*. Michigan: Brotherhood of Theologians Zoe, 1948.

Wright, Norman H. *Making Peace with Your Past*. Ada, MI: Fleming H. Revell, 1985.

Also by Peter Kalellis from Paulist Press

Letting Go of Baggage:
A Journey through Life's Challenges

Kalellis shares insights and practical help for becoming independent and happy by releasing the past, enriching the present, and enjoying the future—the ultimate goal of letting go of our baggage.

Paperback • 978-0-8091-4494-5

Five Steps to Spiritual Growth

Drawing from philosophy, scripture, early church fathers, and contemporary classics, Kalellis speaks directly to the human heart, taking readers on a journey to spiritual growth, beginning from wherever they are right now.

Paperback • 0-8091-4302-X

Saint Paul: The Apostle of Reconciliation

Kalellis shares his always perceptive, and often unexpected, insights into Saint Paul's spiritual adventure. The deeply moving narration is by the author, set against a selection of extraordinary Byzantine art.

DVD • 45 minutes • 978-0-8091-8299-2